D1525247

PRAISE FOR *THE FEARLESS SOCIALPRENEUR*

Dr. Rob Douk conceived, built, and nourished Behavioral Health Works over the past ten years. I have had the pleasure to work with him over the past year as he defined next-step strategies for Behavioral Health Works and several other businesses in his portfolio of companies. This book contains a blend of practical guidelines (principles) married with insight and spiritual guidance (foundations) that he relied on to chart his way through the maze of leadership decisions that were required to build his extraordinarily successful companies. With great craft, Douk weaves his own life story into this entrepreneur's guide and provides insight into how his family's journey around the globe molded his life and businesses philosophies.

—**Marquita Trenier Wiley, MBA**
Mergers & Acquisition Advisor
Founder of Trenier Enterprises, LLC

The Fearless Socialpreneur is an inspirational journal of one man's quest to change the world around him and make it a better place. It is the pursuit of not only the American dream of providing a better life for himself and his family, but something far more significant: a better life for everyone in the world. This book outlines the simple and focused approach of building, maintaining, and growing a business that goes beyond main concepts and bottom lines.

—**Greg Arbues**
Founder & President of the Client Advocate Network
Community Life Pastor of Eastside Christian Church

Dr. Douk is a visionary who sees beyond the here and now and understands how to build businesses and develop tomorrow's leaders. I've witnessed firsthand the value and tangible results that Dr. Douk's foundations and principles bring to an organization's people, process, and product. What he has architected, built, and crafted as the founder of Behavioral Health Works is unmatched in the industry and a testament to his business methodology. *The Fearless Socialpreneur* is a thought-provoking and captivating must-read for any executive looking to unlock the answers of what it takes to thrive in both their professional and personal life.

—Michael Zhe, BCBA

Chief Clinical Officer of Behavioral Health Works, Inc.

If you're looking for the ultimate mentor in today's world, look no further. Dr. Douk is the next business leader and social influencer of our generation. Read this book and you too will have all the tools to make your mark in this world.

—Cary Hokama

Executive Coach & Best-Selling Author of Own Your Self

As an accomplished entrepreneur, Rob offers a practical and clearly defined systematic approach to support and enable entrepreneurs to develop and expand their businesses. His appreciation for the importance of purpose and personal contribution, along with the key elements that comprise a well-designed company, ensures that the reader is provided with a comprehensive approach to reach the next level of success and achieve their goals.

—Dr. Ronit Molko, PhD

Co-Founder of Autism Spectrum Therapies
CEO of Empowering Synergy

As Rob's professor and coach, I am proud to state that his inspirational speech assignment was met with a perfect score. In all my years of teaching, he is the first student that I have given such a score to. As a matter of fact, I continue to use Rob's speech, among other stellar speakers such as Jack Ma and Barack Obama, in my executive business course to provide examples of speakers who display the ability to inspire others. I'm confident that Rob will inspire many through his book, *The Fearless Socialpreneur*. What impressed me most about this man was is his sincerity and passion for others. His comprehension and emotional understanding of others—along with his knowledge of the subject matter—makes what he possesses a rare combination. Every time I use his inspirational speech in my class, I am impressed all over again by this man and his way of inspiring others to do good.

—**Professor Michael Frese, PhD**
Provost Chair & Head of Department at NUS Business School

Dr. Douk's life story is a true inspiration and the quintessential American immigrant experience and dream. His executive and entrepreneurial principles are not only fundamental to any successful business endeavor, but are also timely and momentous in their call for active engagement and contribution back towards community and the greater social good. *The Fearless Socialpreneur* is not just a business book on social entrepreneurship, but also a thoughtful guide on how to create a well-balanced life based on faith, positivity, purpose, entrepreneurship, and service to others.

—**Ljupco N. Fidanovski, MBA**
Finance Executive at Warner Bros.
Founder of E3 Management Solutions

Dr. Douk's ability to engage people through authenticity and passion are a rare commodity and evident in each chapter of *The Fearless Socialpreneur*. His ten principles serve as a daily reminder that while the monetary component of business is important, living a well-balanced life and making a greater impact in the world is within reach if you have the right perspective. As a fellow MBA classmate of Dr. Douk's, I can share that his book is personal with its inspirational story and practical with its ten principles and foundations, making it an essential read for all entrepreneurs and professionals in search of living their fullest potential.

—Robert J. Luna, MBA

Founder & Chief Investment Strategist of Surevest

An inspirational read by an outstanding entrepreneur and dear friend. Attitude is far more critical for entrepreneurs than aptitude in order to survive the rigors of entrepreneurship. Dr. Rob Douk's tireless journey and insights into his success is well documented in his book as he draws inspiration from his life and lessons from his failures. *The Fearless Socialpreneur* is essential for all entrepreneurs who want to be guided by the right values towards prolonged success and happiness. Walk in the shoes of Dr. Douk and learn how anyone who has an idea, dream, or service can share it with the world in a massive way!

—Vicknesh R Pillay, MBA

Founding Partner of TNB Ventures

Asiaone's Top 40 Under 40 Most Influential Asians

The Fearless Socialpreneur

THE

FEARLESS
SOCIALPRENEUR

MAKING IT YOUR
BUSINESS TO **SERVE**
A WORLD IN NEED

DR. ROB DOUK

ForbesBooks

Published by ForbesBooks, Charleston, South Carolina.
Member of Advantage Media Group.

ForbesBooks is a registered trademark, and the ForbesBooks colophon is a trademark of Forbes Media, LLC.

Printed in the United States of America.

10 9 8 7 6 5 4 3 2 1

ISBN: 978-1-946633-03-3
LCCN: 2018933427

Cover design by Melanie Cloth.
Layout design by Megan Elger.

This publication is designed to provide accurate and authoritative information in regard to the subject matter covered. It is sold with the understanding that the publisher is not engaged in rendering legal, accounting, or other professional services. If legal advice or other expert assistance is required, the services of a competent professional person should be sought.

Advantage Media Group is proud to be a part of the Tree Neutral® program. Tree Neutral offsets the number of trees consumed in the production and printing of this book by taking proactive steps such as planting trees in direct proportion to the number of trees used to print books. To learn more about Tree Neutral, please visit **www.treeneutral.com**.

Since 1917, the Forbes mission has remained constant. Global Champions of Entrepreneurial Capitalism. ForbesBooks exists to further that aim by bringing the Stories, Passion, and Knowledge of top thought leaders to the forefront. ForbesBooks brings you The Best in Business. To be considered for publication, please visit **www.forbesbooks.com**.

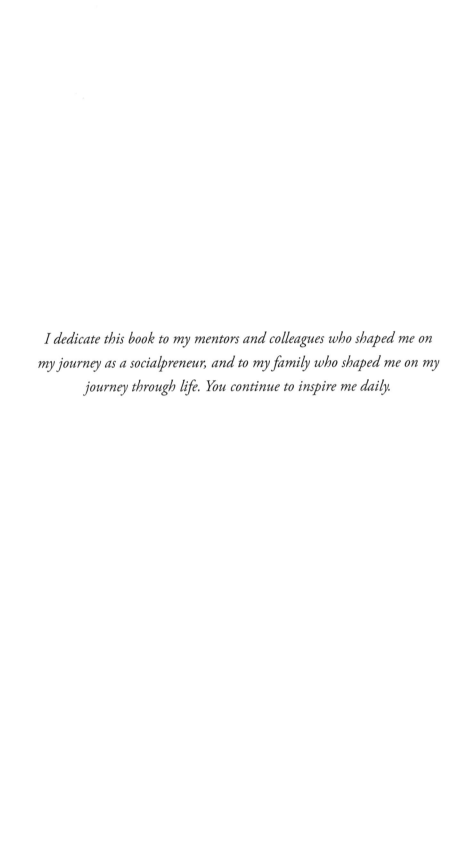

I dedicate this book to my mentors and colleagues who shaped me on my journey as a socialpreneur, and to my family who shaped me on my journey through life. You continue to inspire me daily.

TABLE OF CONTENTS

ABOUT THE AUTHOR. xiii

ACKNOWLEDGMENTS xv

FOREWORDS xvii

A WORD FROM THE AUTHOR xxiii

INTRODUCTION 1
Touching lives

FOUNDATIONS OF A BALANCED LIFE

CHAPTER 1. 17
Faith in a future

CHAPTER 2 33
Family foremost

CHAPTER 3 55
Firm commitment

CHAPTER 4 69
Fitness to serve

CHAPTER 5 83
Fellowship and sharing

PRINCIPLES OF BUSINESS SUCCESS

CHAPTER 6 95

Passion within

CHAPTER 7 105

Purpose to pursue

CHAPTER 8 119

Plan of action

CHAPTER 9 133

PRIME time

CHAPTER 10 165

Paying it forward

CONCLUSION 177

Let's get to work

OUR SERVICES 179

ABOUT THE AUTHOR

Dr. Rob Douk is a clinician turned social entrepreneur and executive coach who is regarded as a thought leader in the behavioral health sector. He has dedicated his career to not only building award-winning businesses but also to transforming organizations whose mission is to provide measurable social benefits.

Dr. Douk is a licensed educational psychologist and a board-certified behavior analyst with a master's degree in counseling and doctorate in psychology. As founder and chairman of Behavioral Health Works (bhwcares.com), he introduced innovative treatment programs and expanded them into regions lacking high-quality services.

A central figure in the social entrepreneurship arena, Dr. Douk is founder of Douk & Company (douk.co), a boutique investment firm that partners with other social entrepreneurs and CEOs. He has co-founded global organizations and serves on several advisory boards. He is co-founder of Hope Out Loud Foundation (holproject.com), a nonprofit dedicated to promoting the well-being of humanity around the world, and of ClinicSoft (clinicsoft.com), a software company that enhances clinical service delivery.

In addition to his extensive clinical training, he received real-world business training from UCLA Anderson School of Management in its Entrepreneurs Program. This experience led him to develop his global business strategy with UCLA Anderson and the National University of Singapore in their Global Executive Dual-MBA program.

Dr. Douk has been named a John Wooden Global Leadership Fellow by UCLA Anderson, and the Silicon Review has honored him among Top 30 entrepreneurs in their 30s. Other honors related to entrepreneurship include the Orange County Business Journal's Excellence in Entrepreneurship award and Cadillac's Dare Greatly award.

An inspirational speaker, Dr. Douk is known to connect with his audiences in a way that motivates them to take action.

ACKNOWLEDGMENTS

They say it takes a village to raise a child. In many ways I feel the same about writing this book. This project is the sum of what I've learned over the years from business mentors around the world, from my failures and my successes, and from starting several businesses from scratch.

I want to thank my God for continuing to open up opportunities for me to pursue. This book would not have been possible without my ForbesBooks team of Bob Sheasley, Eland Mann, and Kirby Anderson, who bring out the best in me.

To the mentors who have shaped me: Your words and teachings have been profound, and your impact has been more than you will ever know. To Ed Salas, for helping me persevere through the pain of starting my first company. To Greg Arbues, for being in my corner through the growth. To dean Al Osborne of the UCLA Anderson School of Management, for polishing the social entrepreneur in me and providing me with the platforms to succeed. And to my family at Behavioral Health Works, from the front-line clinical team to the behind-the-scenes administrative staff—none of this would have been possible without your dedication to premium quality treatment.

Thanks to my parents, who gave me the love and support that every kid needs to thrive. To my brother Brandon, whose mathematical mind is the perfect complement to me. To my sister Michelle, who translates my visions into practice.

To Ami, the love of my life, who empowers me to pursue what truly matters. And to our three children, Sekai Maxwell, Amélie Eden, and Jedediah Neon, who are why I strive to be a better man each day.

FOREWORDS

I got to know Rob very well when he was enrolled in the UCLA-NUS Global Executive MBA program. I was convinced as early as the selection interview that Rob was special. Not only is he an accomplished clinician and a successful entrepreneur who wanted to pursue an MBA, but also a kind and generous person who is sincerely committed to helping people and businesses transform for the better. His professional achievements and contributions speak volumes as man who started life in the United States as a refugee from Cambodia. His success as a leader and entrepreneur is the result of enabling a shared vision through collaboration and inspiring confidence rooted in great respect for humanity and faith in God.

In *The Fearless Socialpreneur*, Rob delivers a pragmatic and powerful treatise on how to design and deliver a sustainable business model that integrates sound management principles and social consciousness underpinned by strong personal beliefs and values. The five foundations, or F's, of a balanced life and the five principles, or

P's, of business success will surely resonate and inspire many entrepreneurs to deliver great business and social value without compromising the important things in life that bring satisfaction and happiness to ourselves and others.

As an educator in the field of marketing for the past 30 years, I have been inspired and guided by the mantra of "learning to teach and teaching to learn." The rich and practical insights that Rob shares validate and inspire other socialpreneurs to embrace learning and sharing for the greater good of business and society. On the concept of "internal brand alignment," which I am passionate about in my teaching and research, Rob underscores this often-overlooked fundamental in managing for success. That is, it is imperative for leaders to align the brand into the corporate culture by connecting the heads with the hearts of all employees so as to build a passionate and high performing organization. This and other insightful organizational learnings are brilliantly discussed in the principles of business success.

Enjoy the book and share it with as many aspiring entrepreneurs who love life and live for the better good of society.

—**Professor Prem Shamdasani, PhD**
Academic Director of The NUS Executive MBA Program
Co-Director of the Stanford-NUS Executive Program in International Management

The Fearless Socialpreneur **outlines the story** of Dr. Rob Douk's tumultuous childhood and upbringing and his hard-earned ascension to success as a social entrepreneur. In his book, Dr. Rob Douk leverages his professional experience as an educational psychologist and behavior analyst to embark on the journey as a social entrepreneur. Filled with spiritual insight and years of personal experience,

Dr. Douk explores how to live a balanced life and the methods to achieve a successful business.

More than a simple how-to guide, *The Fearless Socialpreneur* examines what it means to be a socially conscious businessperson. Everything Dr. Douk works on is for the betterment of society. Whether it's delivering treatment programs to areas without services or promoting worldwide healthcare, Dr. Douk functions with the intent of improving humanity. Through personal experience, Dr. Douk shows how one can create a meaningful life with one foot in the business world and the other devoted to selflessness, faith, and social improvement.

By learning from the insightful tips exhibited in *The Fearless Socialpreneur*, you will discover how to live with a balance between business and ethics.

—Professor Christopher Tang, PhD
UCLA Distinguished Professor & Edward W. Carter Chair in
Business Administration

And so the Dr. Douk and Company adventure begins with the publication of *The Fearless Socialpreneur*! As a behavioral therapist business man, and now social entrepreneur, Douk has set a daunting trajectory for the rest of his life's work: "To launch innovative enterprises that achieve not only financial returns but also social benefits." He believes, and has faith, if you will, in the importance of his evolved purpose. He is passionate and committed to be a person who can inspire others, coach them, serve them, and lead them to produce a more humane society. Douk not only has vision, but he has a plan to touch lives and is doing so in all that he does with determination, clarity, and purpose.

How better then to begin this adventure than by articulating fundamental principles to live a life of purpose and the requirements for business success? His very practical and experience-based philosophy manifests on the pages of *The Fearless Socialpreneur* and within the five F's and the five P's. The first five chapters speak to the foundations of a balanced life and the second five speak to principles for business success. It is not obvious that these two sections should be together, but they work well largely because of the personal anecdotes and lessons that Douk provides throughout the book.

Let me note that *The Fearless Socialpreneur* is not an academic or scholarly treatise. Nor is it the typical five or seven styles of practices for success. This work is different; it is special because it is heavily laced with the personal reflections and experience of its author. Douk expresses himself in a manner which allows the reader to experience the trials and tribulations, and the ups and downs of his life throughout the book. Douk is transparent and honest about his journey from being born in a labor camp in Cambodia and the key lessons learned as a student, a husband, a parent, a boss, and an innovator. Readers begin to feel that Douk is the real deal, authentic, spiritual, and honest. He can be trusted. His voice should be heard.

Not one to stand on his success or accolades, Rob Douk has taken the time to issue a challenge to all of us who imagine a better world. Douk is destined to become the face of a movement of individuals who define success by being able to do well by doing good. And it is the unwavering commitment to improve people and organizations that drives Douk.

Fearless indeed. Turn the pages and learn about a remarkable socialpreneur. Then consider what you can be and do to be part of this coming adventure. How will you harness the F's and the P's to have an impact?

—Professor Alfred E. Osborne, Jr., PhD

Professor of Global Economics, Management and Entrepreneurship

Senior Associate Dean of UCLA Anderson School of Management

A WORD FROM THE AUTHOR

At age 18, sitting alone on the Italian seaside near the terraces of Cinque Terre, I finally understood. Behind me, the village glittered amid the cliffs, but before me lay something grander. I looked to the horizon. It was just me and the sea. It was big and I was small, and yet I was part of it, and it was part of me. I felt silenced, and then filled. I knew in my heart of hearts that someone had authored all of this, and I wanted to follow Buddha, or Mohammed, or Jesus, or whoever that someone might be. I prayed to know the creator.

Backpacking through Europe, I was the quintessential youth out to see the world. I wanted to learn what it was all about. I soon began to get some answers. Strangers at bars would buy me a drink and ask if I had heard the good news of the gospels. On a train to Amsterdam, I chatted with a couple who said they were on their way to plant a church. They told me what their faith meant to them. They seemed, somehow, to love me, though they scarcely knew me.

When I returned home to California at summer's end, my friends threw a big party to welcome me back. Late that evening, I was shocked to see what looked like the face of death on one of the young men to whom I had been particularly close since childhood. His lips were purple, and his skin had turned alarmingly pale, with bulging veins. His body went limp, and he slipped to the floor.

As I rushed to his side and cradled his head on my lap, scenes from our past raced through my mind. I began to pray, as best I knew how. It was more like pleading: *God, really? This cannot be! Turn this around, God. Don't let it end for him this way.* Even as I prayed, I felt panicked and confused. Was this the work of the God whom I was hoping to get to know? Why was he letting something like this happen?

Opening my eyes from that prayer, I looked at my friend, and he was looking back at me, as if questioning me. He was conscious, and the color was returning to his face. I suspected that he had overdosed, but the crisis seemed averted. Nonetheless I needed to get him to his home where loved ones could watch him closely

Driving my friend home on the freeway, I glanced in the rear-view mirror and felt as if the face of evil were scowling at me. "You will not harm him!" I shouted aloud. Then I looked up. I saw a cross, shining brilliantly from a church on the hillside, and I felt peace. That image will be with me always, tattooed into my soul. I knew at that moment that the one whom I was seeking had revealed himself to me. *Come closer,* he was saying, *so that others might know me by knowing you.*

A few hours later, finally alone in my bed, I called my girlfriend, Ami, who later would become my wife. She led me in a prayer, and I invited Jesus Christ into all the rooms of my heart. He had been knocking at my door and waiting patiently. When I finally answered, he met me just as I was. He began walking at my side, guiding me when my steps went astray, pointing to where he would have me go.

Until then I had thought that church was only for the morally polished, for those who could prove themselves to be pure and worthy. As I became involved in the campus ministry at my college, I learned that none of us can ever fit that bill. The church is for the misfits, for the broken ones and the hurting ones, for those who struggle with issues, and hang-ups, and addictions. Hope is for those who need it. I knew then that I needed it, and I know that I need it now.

Each of us walks a different path, and it is not my purpose here to preach—and yet I cannot and must not mask who I am, because it is central to my story. I want you to know me, so know this about me: Faith comes first in my life. To this day, it shapes me. It is at the top of my personal pyramid of priorities. I have come to understand that a magnificent life will not be one in which I pursue my own desires. Instead I must live by God's will so that I might be a blessing for others.

In this book, as we examine ten principles for business and for living, I will share the details of my story, which began when I was born in a labor camp during the Cambodian genocide of the late 1970s.

In this book, as we examine ten principles for business and for living, I will share the details of my story, which began when I was born in a labor camp during the Cambodian genocide of the late 1970s. I invite you to see where I have been and to come along with me as we see where we might go. Successful business leaders and entrepreneurs look beyond the pursuit of profit to see what makes it all worthwhile. At the core of my story, faith plays a huge role as I have followed my parents' example in their fearless pursuit of many endeavors. By creating companies that serve the needs of society, I carry on their legacy.

As a man of business, I have experienced what works and what does not work. I know what it takes to succeed. I know, too, what success requires as a husband and father, as a brother and a friend, and as a child of God. Whatever your faith or creed, you will find in these pages the foundations for a balanced life and the principles for entrepreneurial success. These are truths that transcend. Come with me now and see for yourself.

TOUCHING LIVES

Long past midnight, as I waited at a red light on the strip in Long Beach, California, a car raced up behind me and another screeched to my side. A door slammed, and footsteps slapped on the pavement—and I turned to find the barrel of a sawed-off shotgun inches from my head through my open window.

"Where you from?" a voice barked. I couldn't speak. "Where you from?" he again demanded, louder and shrill. I could see only the gun and, in the glare, the shadowy outline of the angry young man who was thrusting it at my face. He wanted information, and it was cough it up or die.

"You've got the wrong guy!" I managed to croak out, even as he continued to hurl those three explosive words at me, insisting that I explain myself and why I dared to exist here, at this moment, in this place, on this beautiful late summer night.

I again protested that he was mistaken, that I wasn't "from" anywhere—I wasn't a Blood or a Crip or anything of the sort. He clearly was on the hunt for a rival gang member.

Just what was I supposed to say? That I was Rob Douk, and that this was my hometown, and that tomorrow I would be heading off to college to start a new life, dreaming of bigger and better things? *Is this how it's going to go down?* The muzzle of the gun seemed to fill the whole window. *Is this how it is all going to end?* A moment later, the light turned green, and the young man and his gun were gone.

My thoughts raced as wildly as my heartbeat as I drove home. I had been visiting friends that evening, saying farewell to them on the night before my first day at the University of California at Irvine. Still shivering as I tried to sleep, I resolved that I would be saying farewell to this whole scene. *I'm done with this,* I told myself. *I'm out of here! If anyone ever asks me where I'm from again, it sure won't be Long Beach!* I was going places—and wherever I might find the riches of that American dream, it would be a place where you wouldn't have to act tough to survive. Rob Douk was going to make it.

"Where you from? Where you from?" The words still echoed through my being as I finally lapsed into a restless sleep that night. In my dreams, I imagined another interrogation on another warm night long ago in the land where I was born. My father sits tied to a chair, a bag over his head, his ankles bleeding from his shackles. "Where you from?" a thug asks, tightening the bag around my father's neck to choke him. This angry young man wants information, and it's cough it up or die.

This was Cambodia in the 1970s. This was my homeland, a place of hauntingly beautiful landscapes that in those years was beset with unspeakable cruelty. This was where my family was from, and it was from there, from those notorious "killing fields" of the Khmer Rouge, that we escaped when I was one month old. I was my parents' miracle baby, born in a labor camp, and I was their motivation to accomplish what might have seemed impossible.

To this day, my mother and father, who live with me, sometimes awake gasping in the night, trembling from nightmares of being hunted down. What they feel at such times is beyond fear, and it is more urgent than grief. It's primal terror, and it is real to them once again. When I was in graduate school, I stayed for a time with my grandmother to save on expenses, and I often studied till daybreak. I knew that at 3:30 a.m., almost to the minute, her cries would come. The Cambodia that she had known was more than two decades gone, but for her, in the realm of nightmares, it was here and now.

A BOY LEARNS TO SPEAK

Fast-forward with me now to another scene from the past, this one about a quarter century after our Cambodian exodus. By this time, I was a young graduate student majoring in psychology, visiting the home of a two-year-old boy with severe autism who had not learned even the rudiments of speech. I was specializing in a new therapy at the time called applied behavioral analysis, or ABA, which uses no medication. To help pay for my studies, I agreed to regular sessions with the child. Omar was my first patient, and his Egyptian parents had brought him to the United States hoping that someone, somehow, might break through to him.

Arriving for that first session, I greeted this adorable little guy with my best smile—and he greeted me with a barrage of punches. Omar screamed and babbled and spat on me as I tried for two hours, amid his tantrums, to communicate with him. This wasn't going well. As I left, he threw up on me. I felt deflated, having made no headway. This first attempt had been an epic failure, and I felt like one, too. *Was this what I was meant to do for my career? Was I cut out for this?*

At home, I looked in the mirror at the lines on my face, weary from the hours of study, and from too little sleep, and now this disappointing encounter. This is what it's all about, I told myself, not some cozy corner office with a patient lying on a leather lounge. This is raw therapy, two people in a room, trying to make contact, exploring new ways to behave.

> *This is what it's all about, I told myself, not some cozy corner office with a patient lying on a leather lounge. This is raw therapy, two people in a room, trying to make contact, exploring new ways to behave.*

You've got to give it time, I said to my reflection. *This kid is depending on you. Don't give up on him.* I rubbed my eyes, and I pictured my father leading his family through mine-riddled fields to the Thai border. I pictured my mother crouching over me, protecting my body with hers as the bombs rocked the earth. They never gave up on me—and neither had God when I, too, needed to learn new ways to behave.

I resolved to stick with it. I was going to see for myself whether the textbooks were right about ABA therapy. Somehow, I would have to establish a rapport. I would need to understand Omar's motivations and interests. At our second session, as I showed him some of the treasures in my bag of toys, I discovered that he was big on bubbles. He began to show me a different side. As I put the bubbles away, he tapped his hands together, as I had shown him, to sign for "more."

In the weeks ahead, I saw Omar transforming. He was engaging with me, and learning—and then one day a few months later, he spoke his first intelligible words. He had become increasingly interested in the world around him. He had found that he liked not only bubbles but so much else, particularly cars. They fascinated him. He recognized the makes and models.

And he finally discovered yet another wonderful thing, which was language. "More!" he said to me one day. "More!"

I glanced over at his mother, and her eyes were wet. She had seen how much Omar had grown in our time together, but what she might not have seen was how much the therapist, too, had grown. I was learning to let go and stop trying so hard to control how I thought the therapy should proceed. I was learning to go with the flow, letting the child find the pace that worked. I had met him where he was, and stayed by his side while together we went where we both needed to go. Soon, other words tumbled out. "My turn," Omar would say—and it *was* his turn. He was learning to get along cooperatively. He was showing us who he was and what could be.

> *I was learning to go with the flow, letting the child find the pace that worked. I had met him where he was, and stayed by his side while together we went where we both needed to go.*

I met Omar again not long ago, when he and his parents returned to the States for a visit. He smiled broadly at me as I looked up into his eyes—he had grown to be four inches taller than me. He was a high school student in Egypt now, with a circle of friends and a passion for soccer. And he still was fascinated with cars.

My thoughts turned back to that day when I had heard him speak his first words. I had not given up. I had given him, and myself, the time that we needed, and the dividends were evident. That day when Omar spoke had been a turning point for me, as well. That was the day that I became confident of my purpose. Though I had come to understand that I had a passion for helping others, I had been unsure of how I would express that in life. Now I was certain that I would reach out to people as a psychologist, communicating with them, understanding them, turning their behaviors around. And I would be one of the very best, not because I was particularly competitive but because that's how I could help others be their very best, too.

I saw clearly, too, that the hand of God was on my life. He was taking me along his path, not my own, though for years I had not realized it. I discovered my purpose when I began to follow his lead. That is when the course of my career began to make sense to me. My purpose was to journey with my fellow human beings in this way and to make a difference in their lives.

First, though, I'd had to give up my own controlling grip. As an undergraduate, I had studied finances, and newly out of college I had been determined to make as much money as I could. I soon had become disillusioned in my job at an insurance company, despite the tempting salary. I was offered a promotion there, but I felt not the slightest joy in it. I wasn't helping anybody.

God, you designed me, I prayed. *What do you want me to be? If you want me to be a gardener, or an astronaut, or whatever you want, I'll be the best you'll ever see. Just let me know, though. I need to know.* I soon quit that job to pursue my graduate studies.

And now I had met Omar and made a difference in his life. Even though this was a part-time job that paid barely minimum wage, I felt that I was a rich man, finally. Omar had allowed me into his world. In a sense, he was learning to give up his hopeless attempts to control his own behavior and everyone and everything around him, and in so doing, he was finding himself. I had allowed God into my world. I was learning to give up my own hopeless pursuit of what I thought would be the path to happiness—and in so doing, I was finding myself. Omar and I were, in a way, soulmates.

AN INCREDIBLE JOURNEY

Come along with me now in the chapters ahead, and I will tell you more about this incredible journey and how it came about. In short, my family found the way to turn a Cambodian nightmare into an American dream. We migrated from horror into hope. In telling my story, my wish is that I might inspire others to leave behind their own personal horrors, whatever those might be, and head toward the brighter light. I wish to inspire others to do whatever they can to ease the burdens of our fellow humans.

> *My family found the way to turn a Cambodian nightmare into an American dream. We migrated from horror into hope.*

I am grateful that all along that path, my mother and father and the other elders in my family have held tightly to powerful values. Much of what I can offer in this world comes from them, and now it is time to pay it forward, to move far beyond yesterday's pain to promote tomorrow's joy. This is the legacy that I have inherited, and it is the one that I intend to pass to my children and beyond.

We must make the most of the gifts that have come our way. We must take none of them for granted. Those who have taught and mentored me, from childhood through my professional life, gave me the best of themselves. I learned and grew, thanks in large part to good people who overcame adversity and forged ahead in the true spirit of entrepreneurship. They picked up the pieces and made it work, over and over again. They did not succumb to hardship. Instead they found a way to integrate it into a hopeful whole. They showed me how to succeed.

The way to pay it forward is to share those lessons with others so that they might grow. The greatest compliment to a teacher is to teach others in turn. Having been given much, I wish to leave much. This is my responsibility to God and to my fellow travelers on this planet. I want to come alongside others on their journeys, to compare notes, and to move forward to find something even better together. This book is part of my way of paying it forward. Whatever profits come to me from it, I will donate to charity. My goal is to touch lives, and I dedicate this book to that purpose.

FROM THERAPIST TO "SOCIALPRENEUR"

Much of my influence on the lives of others has been through my professional practice, my charitable foundation, and my move to partner with other entrepreneurs involved in socially responsible enterprises.

I am a doctor of educational psychology and a board-certified behavior analyst, specializing in autism and other developmental disorders. In 2009, I founded Behavioral Health Works (BHW), a therapy provider that today has multiple locations, coast to coast, helping families learn to cope with autism and other disorders. A few years after launching BHW, I founded ClinicSoft, a software company that has become an essential tool for clinicians in the field, who must document every step along the path of treatment. That technology, which eases the load of paperwork, was a critical development that allowed me to scale the business while maintaining quality of service to help more people. Today, BHW is looking to venture globally.

My wife, Ami, and I also have pursued other global interests. When it was clear that BHW was on its way to success, we realized that we needed to stay grounded. I wanted to always remember why I got into the field and what mattered most. Ami and I identified that BHW existed to spread hope. It made people's lives better. For many people, hope is a little more than a feeling inside, a whisper that all is well with the soul. We wanted instead to yell hope from the mountaintop for all to hear—and so we founded the nonprofit Hope Out Loud as faith in action. We focused on three initiatives, which we broadly categorized as *health*, *clean water*, and *hope*. Years earlier, when I was graduating from college and wondering what lay ahead, I had imagined how God one day might use me as his instrument to make this world better for his people. I had made an appeal to a greater purpose, and the time had come to be accountable to it.

While receiving clinical training at the Semel Institute for Neuroscience and Human Behavior at the University of California at Los Angeles, I also studied entrepreneurship at UCLA's Anderson School of Management. That led me to pursue my Master of Business Administration degree. I attained a dual Global Executive MBA from UCLA and the National University of Singapore. UCLA named me a John Wooden global leadership fellow in 2015, an honor that commemorates the legendary coach whose value-based style of leadership I admire and embrace. The next year, UCLA elected me to deliver the MBA program's commencement speech.

Meanwhile, I have founded Douk & Co., a boutique investment firm that focuses on social entrepreneurship. Our motto is "pursuing endeavors that matter," which sums up what we do. I identify entrepreneurs who are striving to serve a social purpose. Then I partner with them to help take them to the next level of success. Often, these are CEOs who already have accomplished much but who, for whatever reason, have not reached or sustained the level that I call "PRIME," which I will explain later in this book. As we work together, I share with them my own successes and my own mistakes in striving for that level.

Our relationship is not a typical one of venture capital or private equity. I will not just cut my partners a check for seed money at the outset and hope that they do well. My strategy is hands-on, offering the assistance of my own team. I am not a traditional consultant offering service for a fee, however. Instead, for a percentage of equity, I help my partners to scale up dramatically. My emphasis is on the resources that I can offer to build their infrastructure and promote strategic growth.

> *I help my partners to scale up dramatically ... That growth must be directed toward making an impact in this world.*

That growth must be directed toward making an impact in this world. A broad range of enterprises can meet that criterion, although I choose my partners carefully. These are not limited to the nonprofits and nongovernmental organizations working in the world's trouble spots. They may be software developers or health-care providers, as just a few examples. Sometimes I will help an organization improve its hiring practices or bring in a human resources firm so that it can find the right talent to better fulfill its purpose.

Douk & Co. is another way that I can give back. I understand entrepreneurship. I know what it is like to start something from nothing. I know how to shepherd a company from its birth through its various business stages. As a clinician, it has been my joy to see individuals make progress. That is how I am wired, and now I can find satisfaction in helping people make progress in the business world as well. It is my passion applied to a new purpose. I am still helping others to be their best.

I am an executive coach, but my approach differs from the services typically offered. I share with other entrepreneurs and CEOs what I have learned in business and what I have learned in life—the good and the bad, the mistakes and the triumphs. We must focus first on what is most important, and that means we must sincerely care about one another. Are we taking the right steps, for example, to maintain healthy marriages? Are we spending enough meaningful time with the kids? Are we eating right, getting enough sleep, exercising?

As we build our businesses, we cannot compromise on the foundations upon which that growth should be built. A lack of balance is a prescription for failure. Each of us is a work in progress. As I strive to get my own priorities straight, I share those efforts with my partners and I invite them to share their efforts with me. We hold each other accountable.

I see myself today, in the broadest sense, as a social entrepreneur—or, to use the word that I have coined, a

I see myself today, in the broadest sense, as a social entrepreneur—or, to use the word that I have coined, a socialpreneur. Socialpreneurs launch innovative enterprises that achieve not only financial returns but also social benefits.

socialpreneur. Socialpreneurs launch innovative enterprises that achieve not only financial returns but also social benefits. They strive to capture a movement and to get people's support for a vision and mission. I strongly believe that the future of business these days lies in developing great products and services that will solve societal needs. That could include not only such obviously beneficial endeavors as curing cancer and eradicating the AIDS epidemic, but also technological innovations that enrich our lives and bring us closer together. Socialpreneurs do more than help people in need. They provide the things that people need.

The millennial generation predominates today's workplaces and, in my observation, these young-minded people exhibit a variety of positive qualities including a genuine desire to get behind a purpose or a movement. They have a bent toward doing good in the world. That is largely how they define success, and they bring a great deal of energy to the effort. By pointing that out, I am not discounting the contributions from people of all age groups, of course, and yet the invigorating vitality of the millennials is unmistakable. Their enthusiasm is powerful. They are natural socialpreneurs.

> *I have structured this book in two sections. One is dedicated to the five foundations, or F's, of a balanced life. The second is dedicated to the five principles, or P's, of business success.*

THE FIVE F'S AND THE FIVE P'S

I have structured this book in two sections. One is dedicated to the five foundations, or F's, of a balanced life. The second is dedicated to the five principles, or P's, of business success. As I work with other entrepreneurs, we examine the interplay and the balance of each of those ten fundamentals in our lives. We look through that lens in search of success, and it is a lens that brings clarity and focus. It's the only way to see the real deal. It's the only way to find true satisfaction in business and in life.

When I discuss the five P's and the five F's with those in my own organization who have invited me to do so, I have found that the latter often take precedence in the conversation. If we begin by talking about a business problem, it often leads to a heartfelt discussion of the foundational issues that inform it. We might start out talking about how things are going with the company, and whether we are hitting the numbers, but we often wind up talking about whether we are striking the right chords with

If we begin by talking about a business problem, it often leads to a heartfelt discussion of the foundational issues that inform it.

our families. And so we go deeper, and end up feeling lighter. We connect at a level that allows us to be our best in the business world because we see what it takes to be our best at this business of living.

That is why the section on the five foundations of a balanced life comes first in this book. It is only natural. When I coach other entrepreneurs, the discussion often starts with the five F's. Despite their passion for business, they know they need balance. They are seeking something more meaningful than profits. They are in search of purpose. They want to meet the needs of their communities and their world.

You need not be a person of business or an active entrepreneur to find value in this book. The betterment of the world is everyone's business, and this book is for all who dream of what could be. To those who do run a business or who aspire to do so, let me reassure you that profits come to those who care. Doing good is good business. It pays to be a social entrepreneur. By sharing my journey, and the journey of my family, I hope to encourage others to share theirs. I want to join forces with like-minded souls so that, together, we can overcome.

10 PRINCIPLES OF SOCIALPRENEURSHIP

A Socialpreneur is in business for societal benefit which is implemented through the 5 P's. Equally important is their personal life balance which is addressed through the 5 F's.

Douk & Co. compared the scores of CEOs/Entrepreneurs, based on 10 Socialpreneurship principles, between top CEOs/Entrepreneurs nationally versus Socialpreneurs from Douk & Co.

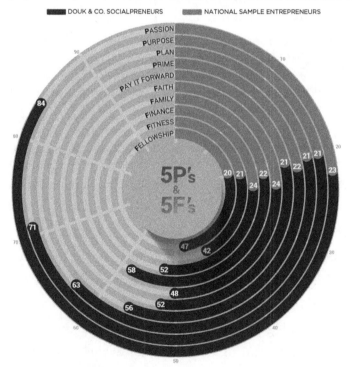

THE ENTREPRENEURIAL PROFILE
Douk &. Co. Socialpreneurs rank as "exceptional" in overall socialpreneurialship compared to the national entrepreneur population.

FOUNDATIONS OF A BALANCED LIFE

The Five Foundations

CHAPTER 1: FAITH IN A FUTURE

CHAPTER 2: FAMILY FOREMOST

CHAPTER 3: FIRM COMMITMENT

CHAPTER 4: FITNESS TO SERVE

CHAPTER 5: FELLOWSHIP AND SHARING

CHAPTER 1

FAITH IN A FUTURE

I awoke to this world in a spray of sunshine and water. In my earliest memory, I am three years old and splashing in a kiddie pool near the avocado tree in the yard of my family's home in California. I feel the radiant joy that all children everywhere deserve to know. I don't remember crying for hours during our family's long flight to New York a few years earlier. I don't remember our days crammed in a Bronx apartment. And I don't remember Cambodia.

My parents do. All too well they remember the Cambodia of the late 1970s. It was there and then that I was born. Cambodia is a beautiful land of rolling, forested highlands surrounding a fertile central plain where the annual flooding of the gentle Mekong for generations has enriched the soil for the rice paddies. To this day, agriculture is central to the way of life, though mostly it is subsistence farming. Millions struggle, but this is a nation of good and hardworking people.

In 1979, however, when my father led his family out of their homeland, Cambodia was an ugly land in the grips of evil. For years, Pol Pot and his Khmer Rouge—officially, the Communist Part of Kampuchea—had waged a guerrilla war from the jungles. He seized power in 1975 after the United States withdrew troops from Vietnam and the Cambodian military government lost its U.S. support. The Khmer Rouge scourge lasted until an invading Vietnamese army deposed Pol Pot in 1979.

Pol Pot's idea of social engineering was to return the nation to an agrarian culture and a classless peasant society. At least two million people—a quarter of the population—perished as the regime evacuated the cities and commenced a policy of forced labor in communal camps. They died of starvation, disease, overwork, and the systematic torture and execution of anyone considered disloyal or a threat. "What is rotten," the regime proclaimed, "must be removed."

Those targeted for extermination included city dwellers, the educated classes and intellectuals (often identified as wearing glasses from too much reading), business owners, ethnic minorities, civil servants, speakers of a foreign language, and those associated with a religion, particularly Muslims, Christians and Buddhists. Pol Pot, in many respects, was his own worst enemy. He came from a relatively affluent family and was educated in the city of Phnom Penh at a Buddhist monastery and a French Catholic primary school. He spoke fluent French. He attended a Paris university to study radio electronics but dropped out as he became intrigued with communist ideology.

The Khmer Rouge also executed former soldiers of the military government, along with their wives and children. Thousands of Cambodian citizens were sent to an interrogation camp to be tortured into false confessions. Many were summarily executed. To save bullets, the killers preferred pickaxes. They smashed children's heads against trees so they would not grow up to avenge their parents' deaths.

My Cambodian name is Dom, meaning *sweet nectar*. I was born two years after my parents met and married in one of those labor camps. They tell me I was their miracle baby and their motivation to escape, one month after my birth—which they did, during the chaos and distraction of the Vietnamese bombing campaign that drove out the Khmer Rouge.

"God, please protect my baby, my beautiful Dom, and I give his life to you!" my mother prayed, clutching me to her chest and hurling herself to the ground to shield my body with hers as a bomb exploded near the Thai border. She lay down her life for me, her sweet nectar, whom she had been trying to keep alive on rice water. She did not yet know the God to whom she prayed, but she understood, in desperation, how much she needed him.

My father lay down his life for all of us. Khmer Rouge guerrillas had captured and held him as a prisoner of war when he was a soldier in the Cambodian military before the fall of Phnom Penh. He managed to endure the torture. The rebels never did learn his identity, and he escaped under cover of darkness, swimming a river and finding his way back to safety. Later, he and my mother were among the millions who were consigned to the labor camps. Now, as a man approaching thirty years old, he would lead us all to safety— his wife and little son, as well as several relatives.

When he speaks of the past, my father tells of humble roots in a remote farming village. There he became quite skilled at working with his hands, and he remains so to this day. He is a reserved and quiet man, but when he reminisces, it is about a life of living off the land and raising chickens and other livestock.

My mother, by contrast, was a city girl who came from a family of relative wealth that had been able to afford maids and a driver to take her to school. She speaks fondly of her father, a high-ranking official, who liked to take his family on beach vacations and picnics to the Cambodian islands. She recalls playing at his side as he stretched out on the sand. This man, my grandfather, was among the first to be seized by Pol Pot's assassins, never to be seen by his family again.

Then came the evacuation. My mother remembers the jeeps rumbling through the streets as young soldiers swept door to door to round up the population for the cruel march to the countryside. Some fled in panic as the troops advanced. Others went willingly, duped into believing that they were being led to safety. My mother recalls shouting at a soldier for treating others cruelly. She might have died on the spot for that infraction—for daring to speak out for dignity. Somehow, she was spared.

My father, too, was spared, and that well may have been due to his farming, fishing, and handyman skills. The camp leaders—who were always Khmer Rouge henchman—deemed him useful for taking care of some of the farming tasks that were unfamiliar to many of the relocated city folk. To some extent, his versatility allotted him a somewhat greater freedom of movement. He could get away by foot on an overnight run to the Thai border, where he acquired fishing nets. Along the way, he paid close attention to the best and safest routes. He would later return to the border to sell his catch. The regime had outlawed money and private property, even jewelry, but my father had a plan and knew that it likely would involve paying people off.

As the Vietnamese began their bombing campaign in 1979, my father recognized that it was now or never. He saw opportunity amid turmoil. He rallied his family as best he could. He led my mother and me to the Thai border and then returned for several others, including his younger brother and his wife, and my grandmother on my mother's side.

The trek was treacherous. Along the way, we lost my mother's youngest sister, too weak from malnutrition and dehydration to go on. Anyone caught fleeing was shot. A bullet shattered my uncle's shin, and the family carried him the rest of the way to the border as he bit hard on a stick to endure the pain. With his fishing proceeds, my father bribed some soldiers to get through. His foresight paid off. In the chaos, however, my father couldn't get back to help his own mother, a sister, and his aunt. His older brothers had already died in the camp.

My father doesn't talk much about those days in the camp, or about the escape. We know what he accomplished, though. Not all of us made it, but we know that it was because of his ingenuity, his courage, and his love that any of us made it. He figured out what needed to be done, and he made it happen. He would exhibit that quality repeatedly in the years ahead. He believed in possibilities.

My parents envisioned and pursued a better life. They had faith in the future and would not give in to despair. I know that it was for me that my parents did this, and for their children and grandchildren who would follow. As my parents fled the killing fields, I was their motivation—this malnourished infant who knew only that he was hungry and who knew nothing of the inhumanity and insanity swirling around him.

The Khmer Rouge had a different take on motivation. The organizers of this agrarian dystopia believed that a starvation diet would compel the people to work harder in the fields and prevent them from becoming fat and lazy. Each worker received one tin of rice every other day. On that ration, they were expected to work the fields from 4 a.m. until 10 p.m. with little rest as armed Khmer Rouge soldiers watched for the slightest excuse to punish and kill. They forbade the starving laborers from partaking of even an occasional taste of the fruits and rice that they harvested. My mother fed me on the water from a thin rice porridge. She waited in a long line to get it.

> *My parents envisioned and pursued a better life. They had faith in the future and would not give in to despair. I know that it was for me that my parents did this, and for their children and grandchildren who would follow.*

Those in my family who survived those times sometimes sit back smiling with their bellies full when we gather for dinner. "See, this is why they didn't want to overfeed us," they say. "Just look what we have become!" Not lazy and unmotivated, however: My family gained the freedom and dignity to thrive.

When my family got to the border, we waited with a throng of desperate people to cross into Thailand. Once there, we were ushered into another camp—but this one was for the refugees fleeing the Khmer Rouge. We stayed there for two years, awaiting sponsorship so that we might move on to a better place, somewhere, somehow. My family has photographs of me during those times. I do not know who took the pictures, but there I am, the miracle baby, standing atop a water barrel and smiling jubilantly. This was my life. I knew no different.

The family stayed for two years in Thailand, but in retrospect the time gave us a chance to adjust to the transition. Humanitarian aid workers educated the refugees on how to survive in their host countries. My family heard stories about some of the refugees who had managed to get an immediate placement. They had learned no coping skills. They didn't know how to use their vouchers, for example, and they felt too intimidated to ask. Beyond that, they did not deal well with the trauma that they had undergone. Some became deeply depressed. Some resorted to suicide.

In response, the sponsorship programs stepped up their attempts to prepare the refugees for what they would face in their new lands. During that time, my parents learned to speak English and how to use a subway and how to navigate the many details of life in other societies. The family had opportunities to relocate to Europe but held out for an opportunity to come to the United States, even though the wait list for American sponsorship was much longer. Meanwhile, they had more time to decompress from the trauma of life under the Khmer Rouge and to become more conversant in English. The family did relocate for a year to the Philippines—it was there that my brother Brandon was born—but soon gained Red Cross sponsorship to migrate to the States.

Our days in the Bronx were relatively brief. The family stayed there only about a year, in a tiny apartment. My parents spent part of their voucher money on a stroller big enough for both my little brother and me. They saw it as an investment in the future. It would allow them to more efficiently interview for jobs and get ahead. It was another example of the attitude that they ingrained in their children: You can find a way not only to make ends meet, but to move forward with faith and a vision for the future. It will work out. We are meant to live life to the fullest.

> *You can find a way not only to make ends meet, but to move forward with faith and a vision for the future. It will work out. We are meant to live life to the fullest.*

My father was leading the family into this new land with the spirit of entrepreneurship, just as he had led the escape from the Khmer Rouge. He did not know God then as he knows him now, and yet God had equipped him for such a time as this.

FAITH OVER FEAR

Faith is the first foundation for a balanced life. Faith is what gets you through as you lean on the knowledge that there is something larger than yourself. When you are faithful, you feel confident that your hopes will prevail even when you cannot see how. Fear does not cripple you.

My family easily could have chosen to give up at many steps along the way. My parents might have conveniently blamed their circumstances and ceased to strive for something better. They might have defined themselves as victimized and powerless. They might have let fear overcome them. Instead, they chose to overcome their fear. They were secure in their faith that the future would be brighter.

On that day when my mother dropped to the ground as the world seemed to be exploding around her, she was not compelled by fear. As she clutched her child, she was determined to protect. She recognized that she must fully depend on something bigger than herself. The leap of faith can be easier when you are at the brink of death and know that you, too, need strong arms around you.

Among the wide variety of beliefs and perspectives that people embrace, the common denominator is this: Faith helps to dispel fears and doubts. It engenders confidence. It motivates us to persist and endure with the spirit of "we shall overcome." I practice a Christian faith that emphasizes that spirit—"blessed is the one who perseveres under trial." Even though they had not yet become Christians, my parents clearly exhibited perseverance in the face of adversity as they escaped the oppressors and as they made their way in those early years with a young family to support. Over the years, they repeatedly demonstrated the power of faith over fear.

As I look back, I see how each of my parents put persistence into practice. My father fought for the family collectively. He calculated the next move at every step. My mother fought for us individually. She made sure, for example, that I gained admission to a safe high school where I could learn and grow without distraction. She was our advocate. My father was our strategic planner. Their strengths complemented each other. Together they were a tour de force of determination that allowed the family to prevail.

Entrepreneurs need that same sense of faith and persistence. They need to lead with a style that makes the most of the strengths of all who are involved in the enterprise. They need to lead with that determination to overcome—because they inevitably will encounter uncertainties and setbacks. If an abiding faith in the future is what builds a strong family, clearly it is also what builds a strong business. It also builds a strong society—and that is why I feel called to work closely with other fearless socialpreneurs who are dedicated to making this world, in some way, a better place.

> *My father fought for the family collectively. He calculated the next move at every step. My mother fought for us individually. She made sure, for example, that I gained admission to a safe high school where I could learn and grow without distraction. She was our advocate. My father was our strategic planner.*

INTO THE BUSINESS WORLD

So much has happened in my family and in the world since those Cambodian days. In the pages ahead, we will replay other scenes from the past to illuminate those intervening years and how my family assembled the pieces to turn troubles into triumphs. Today, I have established enterprises that reach out to people in need.

My first foray into the business world was BHW, which as of this writing has offices across the United States and one in Canada. It took me over two years, however, to launch BHW. Several times I felt that I wanted to give up. As a budding entrepreneur, I experienced for myself the power of persistence. Like my father before me, I had faith that good things would come of my efforts.

This was when Ami and I both were working for the Garden Grove Unified School District—me as a school psychologist, and she as a special education teacher. We were comfortable. Most days we got home at 3:30. We had time to be together as a couple. We were enjoying the sunshine. I kept feeling, however, a calling to do more. I wanted to help others in a bigger way.

Late in 2007, on the eve of what became known as the Great Recession when people lost their jobs and their homes in droves, I began to develop from scratch the business model that I would pursue. I had no templates on which to base my approach to autism treatment. I wanted the program to be unique in its family focus. That is what would separate my business from other providers.

Setting it all up was a painful process, however, in which I had to submit my program proposals, explain my intentions, and define how I would measure progress and issue reports. Meanwhile, I needed approval from state officials, who were not about to let just anybody decide how to best serve the schools. I was looking to set up shop in a way that I could scale it significantly.

To accomplish all that without a framework is difficult. I kept asking myself why I was doing this. Ami and I had secure jobs, after all. Wasn't that enough? With every frustration came a moment of temptation

> *Setting it all up was a painful process, however, in which I had to submit my program proposals, explain my intentions, and define how I would measure progress and issue reports. Meanwhile, I needed approval from state officials.*

when I thought, *Well, I gave it a shot, and that's all I can do.* And then came the day when we learned that Ami was pregnant. Glorious news—but wasn't it about time that I gave up on this business idea? The recession was cutting deep in the economy. Wouldn't the sane choice be to focus on my job and family responsibilities and not some dream that might never come to be?

Once, when I was feeling particularly torn, I met with Ed Salas, a pastor at Newsong Church in Irvine. I was hoping that he would affirm my inclination to give up, that he would tell me I already was doing enough, that this just wasn't the right time. Instead, he led me to clarity. He helped me to map out my journey since birth. He helped me to see the themes of my life. After I connected the dots, I could see clearly again why I was taking this step. I was in tears when I left that meeting with the pastor. In my prayers, I did feel an affirmation, but it was not one of defeat. It was one of persistence. The gentle voice within spoke clearly: *You need to do this, Rob. You need to keep going.*

The doubts would resurface, more than once. I sat alone one evening in the backyard of our home, at the base of a mountain— and that mountain was all that I could see. I again poured out my frustration: God, *this thing is so difficult. I can't take any more of this pain. I feel so rejected. This isn't going to work. They are never going to let me in.*

I heard in response a whisper, calm and confident, the reassuring words of a parent to a child: *It's all right. It will all be worthwhile. You just can't see it now.* I looked up to where the mountain met the sky. The peak was obscured in the mist. I heard again the whisper, as gentle as if it were floating on the breeze: *I need you to continue. I will use you to build something far bigger than you can imagine. Trust me.*

God was holding the door wide open for me. Within a few weeks, I was notified that my program design had been approved.

It was late in 2009, a year that two babies were born in our family: Our first son, and our business. I was learning to be a businessman at the same time that I was learning to change diapers and to be a dad. And all without much sleep: In those early days, until we were sure that BHW would succeed, Ami and I both still held down our full-time jobs, as well.

BHW has grown at an astounding rate. My first office was a single room of 600 square feet, with two small corner desks and a small conference table for training. We soon outgrew it, as well as two other offices. Today, BHW occupies spacious headquarters in Anaheim, a block from the Los Angeles Angels stadium. When I found it, the space had been vacant a few

years. I had been looking for a property much smaller than this one, which was 22,000 square feet, but fell in love with it. I could see the possibilities. I got it for a remarkably good price. The sellers had seen a news article about BHW and were impressed that it was doing good business for a good cause. I drew up the redesign plan myself, ran it past an architect, and personally oversaw the renovation work. I wondered at the time how we would ever make use of all that space. We had parking for sixty-five cars and only needed space for ten. Within just a couple of years, BHW employees were having trouble finding a parking spot. The company already was outgrowing the building—and that was just the headquarters.

Once the business was under way, it all felt so right. I might have bailed at the beginning and convinced myself that this was too risky a move in a shaky economy for a man with a pregnant wife. Somehow, I overcame those misgivings—and I know that the source of that encouragement was the master planner of my life. In his perfect timing, he made it happen.

Like my father, I have learned that you can't wait for your own calculation of the perfect timing. If you keep waiting for what feels like the perfect time to launch a business, you might never start at all. You can always find some reason or excuse to do less rather than more. When you see a clear opportunity, you should seize it and make the most of it. When I saw that the door was open, I walked through it. It's true that it was not the ideal time for us. But it was the right time for us.

> *Like my father, I have learned that you can't wait for your own calculation of the perfect timing. If you keep waiting for what feels like the perfect time to launch a business, you might never start at all. You can always find some reason or excuse to do less rather than more.*

In fear, we doubt, but in faith, we push onward. That's what my father did in 1979, when he was turning thirty years old and a first-time father. And in 2009, when I, too, was turning thirty with a baby of my own, I followed his lead on how to lead a family.

We all need something deeper, bigger, and more impactful that will bring meaning into our lives and inspire us to reach out to the world. Faith in a future helps us to conquer the fears that stand in the way.

Close your eyes. Think about your dreams. What fears are keeping you from reaching those dreams?

Faith and fear are inversely related. The greater your faith, the lesser your fear. How much more might you achieve if your faith consistently outweighed your fears? A lot? At least a little? Or has fear blocked your path? Take a moment to ponder this question, and answer it from your heart.

If you could meet your older self, what do you imagine that he or she might tell you about having faith in the future?

Write your reflections below:

_____

_____

_____

_____

CHAPTER 2

FAMILY FOREMOST

When there was a chill in the air, my mother cooked up a steaming kettle of *kuy teav*, and not just for the family. She made sure we had enough of the traditional Cambodian noodle soup to serve the neighborhood. On the warm days, the yard of our small Long Beach apartment would often be crowded with relatives, friends and neighbors who gathered for rib and chicken barbecues.

It was there, in our little patch of green, where I would climb high in the avocado tree and perch amid the branches to survey my world, the only one that I knew. This was home, and it felt secure. On those streets and in the front yards of the homes of other children— many of them *Khmai* like me but some from other cultures—we played kickball and football until the street lights flickered on. We shot hoops for endless hours against a backboard that my father made from a crate. As season turned to season, our laughter and shouts echoed through the streets.

We lived several years on that block. My family had moved to that area of California in the early 1980s to join a growing Cambodian community there, hoping to gain the support of other immigrants from the homeland that we so recently had fled. Somehow my parents found a way to pay the rent to stay in our apartment rather than in the housing project nearby. To a little boy, our neighborhood seemed like a magical place where the weather was always perfect and everyone was a friend. Such is the perspective of one who knows love.

I later came to understand that my parents struggled financially in those early days. And I know that what sounded like the pop of firecrackers in the neighborhood were most likely not the sounds of celebration. My older friends and cousins would shout that we must take cover. Danger and trouble lurked at the edges of my world, but I only knew that I was happy. I recall those days as a time of freedom and growing and learning. Above all, it was a time when I felt safe in the embrace of family.

Family is the second of the five F's, the second foundation of a balanced life. I was blessed to have been raised in a family that supported me and believed in me. As busy as my parents were, I never felt neglected or ignored. They strived to provide our family with good things—and it's not the material comforts that come first to mind. Rather, my parents' provision was the example that they set as their children grew and learned about life. Like all young people, whatever their circumstances, we were watching. We were seeing the model of the way we should go.

ON A SHOESTRING

As recent immigrants trying to elevate the family lifestyle, my parents worked odd jobs and did their best to get ahead. They wanted to start a business, and eventually they acquired an inventory of athletic shoes to sell at flea markets and swap meets.

My parents would get up at 4 o'clock on weekend mornings before sunrise, and they would load box after box into our two old vans. I remember the warmth of strong arms carrying me, too, out of my bed and into the van, still wrapped in my blanket. And off we went, my parents and little brother and me. The goal was to arrive as early as possible at the market and to get in line for the best possible spots. There, amid other vendors selling a multitude of goods, we would set up our tables and tarps and proceed to peddle our shoes.

And by *we*, I mean all of us. Even at just eight years old, I was helping customers choose their best fit. Our shoes were quality name brands, not the knockoffs that some of the other vendors were peddling. I was usually paired with my mom at one booth, and my brother with my dad at another. I observed how she greeted people and negotiated with them. I saw her offer great deals to customers who deserved them, and I saw her stand firm with anyone being unreasonable. I learned what worked and how to conduct business effectively. Once, when my mom sent me to buy some socks, the vendor afterward told her how proud she was that I had stood my ground and insisted on a good price. I discovered that I loved to watch people, and I had eight to ten hours each day to do just that.

To earn my own wage was a satisfying experience. My parents gave my brother and me each two dollars to spend. One dollar was for lunch, and often we would split a Cinnabon and a hot dog or sometimes a churro. The other dollar was for whatever we wanted to buy, and what we wanted was baseball cards. We were avid collectors.

We often spent our lunch breaks sampling the video games for sale at the corner shop. We hooked a hoop to the back of the van and played basketball. Every weekend seemed like a family outing. I'm sure we were having more fun than a lot of kids who stayed home on Saturdays to watch television. Even as I helped to load all those boxes into our small van so they would all fit, I imagined I was playing a game of Tetris.

We spent most of our time, though, manning the booths, and there I learned the elements of salesmanship and found that I had a flair for it. I never tried to push a sale. I tried to read the customers' needs and genuinely educate them about the best products. I found that I could size up people and which shoe they would choose, based on how they were dressed and their mannerisms. I could tell who was the outdoorsy type, who was athletic, and who just wanted to be hip and stylish. I helped match them with the product that would be best for them. I truly wanted to help the customer, not just move the product.

Along the way, I made friends with those around me, including the other vendors and the regulars. I liked to hear their stories and how they got to where they were. It was a time when I could soak everything in. I didn't have to rush anywhere. I could just be in the present and in tune with my surroundings, with no agenda other than to just exist in that time and place and to be a kid. I gained a lot from those years at the flea markets and swap meets. I learned about people and the dynamics of how they behaved and interacted. I learned to appreciate them and to respect their differences.

As I manned the booth, I found that I could connect with others easily and understand them. I found satisfaction in helping them however I could. To me, a big part of selling was educating. Once a customer could see the benefits, the merchandise sold itself. The right fit was essential: high tops for the basketball player, low tops for the runner.

I learned to add value by explaining the new technologies and innovations and how they addressed the customers' specific requirements. To customers, the added value translates to a good deal. Sometimes I could help them understand a need that they had not yet recognized. Whenever you can help someone address a need or solve a problem, he or she will appreciate you—and I quickly learned that an appreciative customer is one who will spread the word. Good service is the best promotion. It's simply good business.

I studied shoes. I wanted to be an authority, and my parents appreciated the value of that knowledge. During the weekdays, we would go to the wholesale camps to purchase shoes. As I got older, I had a voice in selecting what would sell. How did I know? Because I had been studying not only shoes. I had been studying people, too. I could see in their eyes the moment when they were convinced that one pair of shoes was better for them than another, and I could tell just what had led them to that point of conviction.

"THE VANS ARE GONE"

My parents saved diligently so that they could purchase that inventory of shoes. They weren't acquiring them on consignment; they were buying them at a wholesale price, so they were on the hook for them until they resold them at retail. To get to that point, they worked at a variety of jobs.

They did so well selling the shoes at the flea markets that eventually they were able to open a storefront at Seventh and Broadway in Long Beach. It was at a premium location, one store away from the corner. No longer were we selling at weekend flea markets.

We devoted full-time to that store—but only for about a year. My parents had been misled by a clause in the rental contract, and when they realized what was going on, it was too late to stay. They had met an attorney through their employment who reviewed their lease agreement and did his best to help them, but the news was not good. They had to be out by midnight. My parents frantically moved their inventory back into the vans late into the night.

And so after that year on Broadway, it was back to the weekend swap meets, along with a midweek market in La Mirada on the grounds of a drive-in theater. Meanwhile, my parents picked up jobs during the week while replenishing their shoe inventory for the weekend market, usually on the parking lot of the Orange County Fairgrounds. It was an upscale area near the beach, and the market attracted relatively affluent shoppers who strolled the grounds looking for good deals on some cool products while getting a nice tan.

Then came another dark time for our family. One morning, we arrived at the fairgrounds a little later than usual and were unable to get a spot to unload our inventory from the vans—and then the skies opened in a cloudburst. We dashed for cover, and while we were eating breakfast my father came running up to us. He was soaking wet, and his face looked drained.

"The vans are gone," he said—four innocuous words, but alarming in context. I was 12 and old enough to grasp the gravity of the situation. That day is a blur in my memory, but I recall my father's gestures and the lines on his face as he told the security workers and the police about our plight. Could they *do* something, anything? The cargo on those vans represented the family's life savings. And it had vanished, all of it, never to be recovered. Somehow, we got back home that day, bone tired, dejected, our clothes drenched. My mom sobbed for days.

IN THE HIGH DESERT

Once again, my father found a way. Scraping together whatever savings he could, he began to prepare for a new venture to support the family—a 99-cent store, where nothing would cost over a dollar. He managed to set aside enough to buy a starter inventory, and he found an affordable lease on a storefront in the high desert town of Phelan, ninety miles to the north on the other side of the San Gabriel Mountains and several miles from the Mountain High ski resort. It's a low-income area, so he figured a 99-cent shop would do quite well—and it did. He built up the inventory to carry a variety of household goods and sundries.

To provide a home for us, he bought a small towable house trailer. I went with him into the mountains, near the town of Wrightwood, and listened as he negotiated with a man for the best price. It was an old trailer that had seen better days, but it would do. It had a cabin with one bed and a sofa in the kitchen that converted into a second bed. This was to be our new home.

My dad arranged to have the trailer towed out into the desert to the property of a couple, Madeline and George, whom my parents had befriended soon after opening the store. They had been among the early customers, and upon hearing our story they generously offered to let us park the trailer on their land, where they kept a few animals and, to my delight, a cute little puppy. We showered in their house and slept in the trailer.

Such were our accommodations as I entered my first year of high school and ambled into adolescence. After school, in the late afternoons while my parents were still busy at the shop, I watched over my little brother Brandon. We would shoot hoops together and dine on microwavable taquitos and cheeseburgers.

My baby sister was born during our desert days. When she was about two months old, we awoke one morning to find the ground covered with snow. Never before had I seen snow. It felt like another world. All five of us went out to play in it, catching the flakes on our tongues as it fell and throwing snowballs. The scene is etched in my memory, a tableau in time. We were family, and we were together.

Sometimes my brother and I would man the store while our parents went "down the hill" to the Los Angeles area to pick up supplies. This region of the high desert was rather backward, and a lot of the locals were not used to seeing people who looked like us. Some had never ventured beyond the desert. Young people occasionally would come by on skateboards, bang at the shop door, make obscene gestures, and throw rocks at the windows.

The racism was palpable in the community. Such incidents happened more than once, and we didn't always tell our parents about what had happened—but when we did, they were deeply concerned. Our mother in particular worried that Brandon and I, who were growing into proud young men, would get into fights. "Would you like to go back to Long Beach?" she asked one day, and my brother and I both nodded. We had been there only about a year.

THE BONDS THAT ENDURE

And so our parents sold that store. They made enough of a profit that my mother didn't have to go back to work after that. We packed our bags and crossed the mountain to go "home." Our parents wanted us to spend our high school years in a community that was more diverse and where we could feel a greater sense of support. They wanted us to find our own direction and not feel trapped into a life of running the family store. That was not the future that they wanted for us. And besides, the rest of our family was back there, and they wanted the support of relatives, as well. They wanted their little girl to know her grandma and her aunts and uncles and cousins.

I do not mean to suggest that our year in the desert was a bad one. The racism was undeniable and yet somehow it seemed incidental. I made some good friends there and left with some enduring memories. What really held it together for my brother and me was our participation in sports. Basketball was our common passion. Brandon, in fact, who was in middle school, was a rising star. All the coaches were talking about him. I never felt discontented or embarrassed about our circumstances. I felt no bitterness that this was all we had. I had everything that I needed. I'm sure I had my rebellious moments, but I respected my parents. They were busy people indeed and couldn't get to our basketball games, but they loved us nonetheless.

As for George and Madeline, they felt like another set of grandparents. They were dear, sweet people who treated us well. I had always wanted a pet but had never been able to have one—and that was the year that I got to take care of their puppy. His name was Murphy, and I would put him in my bicycle basket and take him for rides. At times, I would overhear Madeline sharing the gospel with my mother—in fact, that was probably the first time I had ever encountered the message. It would still be some years before my mother embraced Christianity, but I do believe the seed was planted during those conversations with our dear hostess. At one point, I accompanied a friend to church, a new experience for me.

The birth of our sister was a true blessing for our family. My father carried her picture on his keychain. This little one became his motivation to pursue greater things, my mother says as she recalls those days. Years earlier, in another land, she had ushered me into the world—and I had been his motivation then. Once again, as in Cambodia, he found himself responsible for the well-being of a new life. He was determined to do his best at this job called fatherhood.

> *As I look back, the prevailing theme of those years—and of the years since—has been the power of family bonds. We supported and learned from one another. As much as I needed my parents, I found that they needed me, too.*

As I look back, the prevailing theme of those years—and of the years since—has been the power of family bonds. We supported and learned from one another. As much as I needed my parents, I found that they needed me, too. Sometimes it was a practical matter: At times they leaned on me, even when I was a young boy, to be their interpreter and negotiator. They recognized the importance of a strong command of English, and I could help them fill the cultural gap when necessary. Their greatest need, however, was to love and to be loved. We were family, and that fact alone propelled them to do their best.

In observing my parents, I learned the fundamentals of becoming an entrepreneur long before I headed off to college for advanced degrees in psychology and business. They were entrepreneurs in Cambodia, in the Bronx, in Long Beach, and out on the desert, and they have continued that pattern in the years since. And they raised entrepreneurs. Their three children were watching, and they saw that it was good.

The bonds of family must be a priority in the life of an entrepreneur. That was the case for my parents, both in their homeland

and in their new life in America. Those in my family who made it out of Cambodia stayed together afterward, from Thailand to the Philippines to New York to California. When all you have is family, the bonds grow tighter. We were committed to unity.

Sometimes, success comes at a price, and loved ones start to drift apart. That is the true tragedy. No amount of money or material wealth can overcome that. I often think back to the days when our family had next to nothing. All in all, how happy we were.

SNAPSHOTS OF MY FAMILY

Let me tell you more about the people with whom I have been doing life. They are the loved ones who are closest to me and who are traveling with me at every step of my journey—my wife, my parents, my grandmother, my siblings, my children. I have already introduced you to some of them. Here I want you to see up close the role they play in my life and the power of those relationships. As I share these snapshots with you, think of your own family, however you define it. Mine is a family in the traditional sense, but yours may be quite different. What matters most are the bonds of love.

What matters, too, are the bonds of trust. You will notice that in many ways my immediate family is intertwined with my business world. I want these people around me because, in truth, others could not offer as much in those positions. Credentials matter, certainly, and so does a foundation built over years together. I value the transparency of my relationship with family members and how that translates into confidence that they will execute their duties to their utmost. I know that they care as much as I do. We can talk openly and frankly about what is working and what is not, and they have saved me from making some big communication mistakes. They hold me accountable. That is not to say that I do not have that relationship with other associates, but with my family it is a given—and that's just good business.

Relationships matter both off the job and on the job. I have hired people with all the right letters after their names, men and women who have worked for Fortune 500 companies, and they often do quite well—but I have shared with them that they must do well not just as individuals. Those around them must be growing, too. Those are the people who exhibit the kind of energy that leads to promotions. They care not just about their own success but the success of their colleagues. Nobody can work in a silo. Individuals and departments must support one another. A successful career must involve more than a series of business transactions. It must be relational—and that is why I am focusing on the five F's before the five P's.

My father

My father's Cambodian name is Sriv, but he adopted the name Paul after immigrating. He is a doer, not a talker. I experience his love through his gifts of service. He never needs to tell me how he feels. He demonstrates it. That is his way.

Once, for example, he helped me make a triptych to display my sixth-grade science project. All I really needed was cardboard and tape, but he showed me how to make the panels from wood and hinges. His message to me was clear, though he communicated it not through his mouth but rather through his hands: *The way to succeed, son, is to always offer your best.* As we worked together out in the yard, he showed me the meaning of "measure twice, cut once." We kept at it, even as it started to rain, until the project was done. My heart felt so full that I thought it might burst.

He is good with his hands. His nature is to make things happen and to fix what is broken. Some would describe him as a *MacGyver*—we affectionately call him a *KhmaiGyver*—but he's far more than a fix-it man. He is resourceful and persistent.

Before he became a soldier, a village elder told him that bullets would not find him, and that in time he would meet and marry a woman with a mark above her knee. "Your dad was hot stuff," an aunt in Cambodia told me once when I visited there. "There were girls from different villages who would chase him home." But he wasn't the type to play the field. He was looking for his lifelong love, and it was his persistence that finally won over my mother after they met in the labor camp. He was determined to win the heart of this hard-to-get woman who was "out of his league," she says with a smile. Perhaps he knew she was the one because she had a scar above her knee, the result of a moped accident when she was a child. They married within a few years, finding hope amid the devastation, and I came along two years later.

My father is not a man who takes shortcuts. He attends to the details and acts with precision. At times his exacting nature has frustrated me, but I see now how it served the family well. He makes sure that he is building on a solid foundation. He does his best to ensure that things go right the first time.

I helped him once to lay new tiles in a room that he was renovating, and he insisted that we scrub the old floor clean before tearing it up and starting anew. *Why?* I didn't know, then. But he knew full well. He didn't tell me, he showed me: *This is an opportunity to do it right from the start. Don't allow the old dirt to spoil your new work.*

He is a quiet man but a solid and powerful presence in the family. He is a rock in our lives. When he is proud of me, I know. He doesn't pour out his feelings. He doesn't wax poetic. He will simply say, "Good job, son." And he'll pat my back. To me, that feels the same as if he had shouted, "I love you!"

My mother

My mother, whose American name is Amanda and Khmer name is Socheat, is a planner and an organizer—you might think of her as a Khmer version of a Martha Stewart. She cares deeply about the aesthetics of her world and her household, keeping everything in place and smelling pretty.

Even during tough times, my mother had a way of making us feel that we had everything we needed. Even when we lived in a trailer, life felt complete. I credit her for that perspective. She lives life to the fullest, and she is clear about her feelings and her beliefs.

Like the other members of my family, she became a Christian. For her, it was a pragmatic decision. Recognizing that all her children had embraced the faith, she too put her trust in God. She said that she wanted to go to the same heaven as her kids. After she became a believer, my father did as well.

My mother is the eldest of five siblings who made it out of Cambodia during those dark years. Two brothers and two sisters also survived the Khmer Rouge oppression. As the family fled, she lost her youngest sister, who died of a waterborne disease and dehydration.

She has always served as an outspoken advocate for her family. She is passionate about life, and she stands up for the causes she believes in and looks out for the best interests of others. I have come to recognize that we are much alike, she and I.

My grandmother

When I was small, my grandmother (American name, Jamie Ou; and Khmer name, Ou Sophat) was the caretaker for my brother and me as well as our cousins while our parents were working. She did a phenomenal job of keeping us safe and healthy as we spent many days together in the California sunshine.

It was her influence, primarily, that led me to become fluent in speaking Khmer, the Cambodian language. In those days spent with my grandmother, I learned much about the culture of the land where I was born. We became very close, and I was blessed to get to know her even better as an adult when I lived with her for a few years while I attended graduate school. Today she continues to be an active and independent spirit.

My wife

Ami is my angel, and she has been the spiritual one who has had a deep influence throughout my family. Her charm and her sweet, contagious smile seem otherworldly. She has a free and positive spirit. She's like the girl next door, without an impure thought in her head. I love her beauty, and I also find it charming that she can be a bit clumsy at times. Ami might not come across as the smoothest of souls, but people are drawn to her. Even strangers have been known to share their deepest feelings with her soon after they meet, such is the openness of her nature. She exudes warmth.

Ami understands the power of family bonds and why they are so important as a building block in life and in business. In fact, that was part of what attracted her to me. After we met in college, she soon came to deeply appreciate my family's emphasis on structure and security and togetherness, no matter what chaos surrounded us. She thinks of my parents as hers as well, and she has talked with them in depth about their pasts and their inner lives. And she enjoys them for who they are. She finds it delightful, for example, to accompany my father to the hardware store to pick out the parts to fix something around the house. Her attitude has helped me to appreciate my parents even more.

My brother

Before my brother Brandon was born, my father had a dream that he was given a prince—and the word for that in Khmer is *Bot*, which is Brandon's birth name. My brother is a remarkably good behind-the-scenes player. He calls me his Batman, and he is happy to be my Robin. He wants me to be the Michael Jordan, and he is happy to be my Scottie Pippin.

We get along well. He wants me to cast the vision, while he executes it superbly, although he also works independently exceptionally well. Brandon is a big reason that I can succeed. He has been with me in business day in and day out. He has stayed at my side when I have worked into the morning hours. He has always been there for me. Like our father, he is very resourceful and he is the quiet type, the rock, the strong and reliable foundation.

In a lot of ways, he is my best friend as well as my brother. Growing up, we shared a love of basketball and other sports, and we collected baseball cards together. Today we share a love for golf. He is a man who gives it his all, whatever his endeavor. His interest in golf has led him to an encyclopedic knowledge of the sport and the clubs. When he was into mountain biking, he displayed the same devotion, making it much more than a hobby. When we were children, he had an expert's grasp of the shoes that we were selling at the flea markets and the store.

Brandon is also very loyal, and that too is a quality that I have seen in him since we were kids. He is committed to whatever he is doing, and to those with whom he is doing it. He met his wife, Denise, at BHW, where she was a therapist at the time—in fact, she was the second one whom I hired. Today they have a beautiful little daughter. He became chief finance officer at BHW, a position well-suited to his mathematical brain as opposed to my more abstract thinking. He is dedicated to family and to career and to the Christian path that his family is walking.

My sister

Although she is my baby sister, born when I was a teenager, I think of Michelle as an old soul. She is young in appearance, but she seems to carry within her the wisdom of ages. Her Cambodian name, Moich, is just an endearing term that certainly fits someone of her sweetness. I see in her a hard worker who tends to be a homebody and a quiet sort—and so in that way she is a lot like our father. She also shares our mother's organizational skills and her feminine appreciation for those things that smell good and are pretty.

As director of operations at BHW, Michelle became adept at developing projects, translating them for everybody to understand and execute. Thinking in terms of spreadsheets and timelines, she proved herself to be highly dependable and skilled at the logistics. She approaches her career as she approaches life—with thoughtfulness and sensitivity. Because she is naturally empathetic, she understands other people's perspectives. I often have seen how readily Michelle comes to understand the needs of others and what they really are trying to communicate. I value her maturity and her insights.

I find her to be a great interpreter. Her approach falls somewhere in between my abstract thinking and our brother's mathematical mind. She can hear my visions about where we should focus during the next quarter, and she will tell me either, "You already have too much on your plate, Rob" or, "Yes, and here is how I think we best can accomplish that"—and then map it out and work with the team to get it done. Because she understands me so well, she helps me to explain and communicate the vision.

Our older son

In 2009 when Ami and I were focusing our prayers on the needs of humanity, we brought Sekai into the world. In fact, his name in Japanese means *world*. His middle name, Maxwell, connotes great leadership. We envision him growing into a man with a heart for the world. He is a leader indeed. All his little cousins want a haircut and shoes just like Sekai's. He seems to naturally attract others, and they want to follow his example.

When Sekai was two years old, my father was babysitting him one day when he noticed that the little boy was praying. He listened. Sekai was asking the Lord to help the victims of the Japanese tsunami. It was then and there, my father says, as he witnessed a child's earnest entreaty, that he fully understood in his heart that there was a God to whom he could pray.

In many ways, Sekai is similar to me. So that I don't make him out to be some wise little old man, let me point out that he is quite a prankster. In school, he gets good behavior awards, so he knows how to compose himself, but when he gets home he unleashes his energy. Generally, though, he does have a stable and calm demeanor, and he is careful and thoughtful in his approach. He has remarkable patience for building Lego masterpieces, for example. He stays with his project and focuses until it is complete, and then puts it on a shelf and becomes a completely different kid, unwinding and having a blast. Like me, he loves sports. He seems to enjoy the activities that I enjoy, and I do believe we are wired much alike.

Our daughter

When Ami and I were dating, one of the first movies that we saw together was the French film *Amélie*. We fell in love with that character, even as we were falling in love with each other, because she was so cute and so giving and yet feisty. If we ever had a daughter, we agreed, we would name her Amélie. And so, in 2011, it came to be.

Her middle name is Eden, as in the beautiful garden before the fall. She has lived up to her name. She loves everything beautiful. Amélie is very thoughtful, as well. She makes cards for people when she knows that they are sad or not feeling well. That is also an expression of her artistic and creative nature, which she gets from her mom.

She is a happy little girl and wants to be around happiness—in fact, she has been working through her emotions in facing some of the things at school that make her sad. We are breaking the news to her, little by little, about the ways of the world, but as much as we can we want to preserve that pure and beautiful spirit. Amélie embodies sweetness and strength—and her nature is to nurture. Once, after I nearly severed a toe in a surfing accident, she was nearly a constant companion at my bedside, offering new bandages and showing the sincere concern of a four-year-old.

Our younger son

We call Jedidiah Neon our "cherry on top." His first name means *friend of God*, and his Cambodian middle name means *insightful*. We see him as our insightful friend of God.

Jedediah, born in 2015, is a true outdoorsman, taking after both Ami and me. When I was his age, I too enjoyed the outdoors of the Thai refugee camp, such as it was. Jedediah likewise wants to be outside all the time. We can take him to the beach and give him a towel and his bottle, and he will be the picture of contentment. In fact, he's content if we take him virtually anywhere. He's an easy baby. He naps well, then wakes up smiling ear to ear and waving to everyone in sight. It's what he does. At church, he dances and sways to the music and lifts his hands to God. He is a social spirit with a deep caring for others. "Are you okay?" he often asks.

TO WHAT END?

You could rise to the heights of business success, but if you lose your family while doing so, what have you profited? You could gain a fortune, but what does it avail you? To what end are you laboring? As we make our way in this world, striving for the good life however we define it, we must always remember the sanctity of our homes. Our families need us. Our children want our time. They don't need more money, and they don't need more apps on their iPads. They need caring and sharing parents.

> *You could rise to the heights of business success, but if you lose your family while doing so, what have you profited?*

As I was building my business, a wise advisor, Greg Arbues, told me this: "The best return on investment that you will ever have is time with your children. Never forget that." And I haven't. It can be tempting, when there are big decisions to make and the work and the deadlines are pressing in, to attend first to those matters that seem so urgent. Generally, they are less important than playing catch with your child. If you build an empire but your children do not know you, what is the worth of such a kingdom? Your castle is a cold place. We must be careful how we measure our accomplishments.

Material success can get in the way of true success. Many children grow up feeling discounted or abandoned. Their parents have allowed their own pursuits, as worthy as they might seem, to dilute their time with their family. They fall short on their first and foremost duty as shepherds of the family. True, to be a good provider is a serious responsibility—but a wise leader strives for balance. There are many who have built fortunes but failed with their families, and many others have struggled financially and yet their families will forever feel fortunate indeed. It's all in what you count as riches.

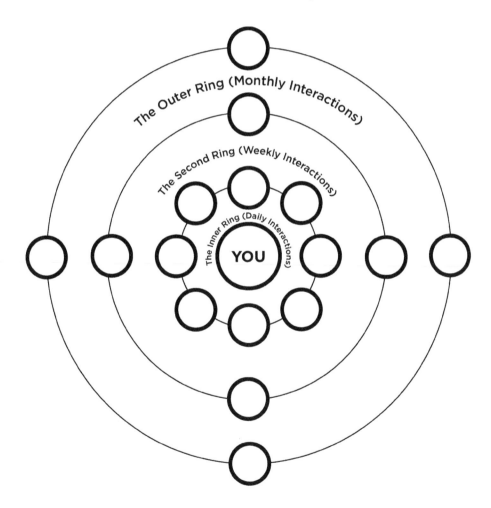

The nucleus: You

The Inner Ring *(Daily Interaction): Family Members*
Time Required / Week: ~30 hours / week

The Second Ring *(Weekly Interaction): Closest Friends*
Time Required / Week: ~4 hours / week

The Outer Ring *(Monthly Interaction): Mentors & Old Friends*
Time Required / Month: ~ 4 hours / month

CHAPTER 3

FIRM COMMITMENT

On a date with Ami recently in Manhattan Beach, we sat on the pier watching the breakers come in and the surfers doing their best to ride the waves. One young man was particularly steadfast. Pummeled repeatedly, he kept going back for more, determined to get it right, scanning the horizon for the next best opportunity sweeping in from the wide Pacific. Time and again, he climbed back on his board.

I thought of my father. Though surfing is not his sport, he has always gotten back on board even in the roughest of seas. He, too, has watched for the waves coming in, riding them to the best of his ability until they overcame him—and then righting himself and getting ready for the next break, the one that would bring him gliding smoothly shoreward. My father has long recognized the cycles of life.

He faced the setbacks, waited for the right timing, and turned them around. He did it in Cambodia. And he did it, time and again, in America.

My thoughts turned, as well, to the waves that I too have experienced, the cycles of life and of business. Some of those waves are deep and powerful swells, and others are weaker and quickly run their course. The question is this: Which wave will lift you the highest? Which will send you soaring to your destination?

After our year in the desert, when my parents sold their store and we moved back to Long Beach, my father started a delivery company as an independent contractor. He did phenomenally well. I recall my mother mentioning proudly at one point that he was earning as much as a doctor. His business flourished to the point that several of our relatives joined his fleet of services, and that is their livelihood to this day.

After a few years of developing that enterprise, he took note of the ascendant real estate market and began to flip homes—a natural progression for one who is handy with a hammer. He operated the delivery service by day, and he put his renovation skills to good use in the evenings and on weekends. For his first purchase, in Corona, he got a loan with the help of the equity that he pulled from our Honda Passport for a down payment. That property nearly doubled in value in less than a year.

Then one day, as he was driving alone making a delivery, a car slammed into his vehicle. The rescue crew had to saw through the wreckage to set him free. He recovered, although he would have lingering back issues. Little was left of the passenger side, and anyone sitting there would not have stood a chance—but that seat was empty. My brother sometimes joined him on long trips but had been unable to accompany him that day.

On his keychain that day, our father had his little girl's photo, the one he had carried with him since our days in the desert. He had it with him all the time that he was building the delivery service. He said that whenever he looked at her photo, he would feel a renewed energy to keep on driving the routes. She was his reason to keep on keeping on—and in the days and months ahead, he would need even more of that motivation as his hurting body healed.

He was unable to drive, and the medical bills were piling up. A friend took over his routes for a few months and donated the money to him. It was a huge help—and such largesse demonstrated just how much his colleagues truly liked this man. I was out of college at that point and had taken my first job working in corporate insurance, where I was learning the ins and outs of coverage for disabilities and work injuries, so I was able to help him navigate those issues.

It was a stressful time for the family, but it was also a time of encouragement and commitment, as we supported and complemented one another with our various strengths and skills. That's how it is in a strong and caring family, and that's how it is in a strong and caring business. Doors were opening and opportunities were beckoning. Sometimes only in hindsight can you see such things.

Our dad, once again, got on board. He increasingly turned his attention to his other source of income—his real estate dealings. With my newfound business acumen, I assisted with that, too, helping him to scrutinize the contracts. He flipped houses for years until retiring. Paul Douk, the ultimate entrepreneur, the builder of several businesses, was at it again with a firm commitment to succeed. Retired now, he and my mother share our house as part of the nuclear family, and today they focus on their grandchildren and their nonprofit work around the world.

"YOU'LL JUST HAVE TO BE A GOOD RUNNER..."

As I was progressing through my final three years of high school, I began to think about my upcoming college career. I believe that I needed education to take me places, and to avail myself of every opportunity I hoped to enroll in SAT preparation classes. My parents looked into the possibility but decided it was too expensive at that point for the family budget.

My mother broke the news to me, and she might have expected that she would need to reassure me that it would be all right, but I was the one who reassured her: "I remember you telling me, Mom, that I might not have the shiny new bike like the other kids but we could get to the same places. 'You'll just have to be a good runner,' you told me."

It was lesson on perseverance and resourcefulness. She had wanted me to know that I must not feel handicapped by life. I was just as good as anyone else and had a right to pursue opportunities. I could attain anything if I committed myself to the endeavor and wanted it badly enough. She and my father had been demonstrating that lesson for years, as they built and rebuilt. I had seen them launching new businesses and making them work, against the odds.

In those days, I wanted to make a lot of money—because wasn't that the American dream? I spent much time in pursuit of shiny things. Eventually, one comes to understand that success can be defined otherwise. I wasn't going to get ahead because of worldly things that were given to me. Success had to arise from within. Abundance would not be the making of the man. The making

Success had to arise from within. Abundance would not be the making of the man. The making of the man would bring abundance.

of the man would bring abundance. Live an honorable life, and all those shiny things would be added.

My parents equipped me with the tools to get started. I knew that I would make it if I put my mind to it. I might have to run, but I could do it. I knew that I could get to college. I knew that I could make money. I knew that I could launch a business and have my own firm—if I had a firm commitment.

BRINGING LIGHT INTO DARK PLACES

The third foundation of a balanced life is "firm commitment." In any chosen career, you need to give the proper perspective to whatever you are building—your practice, your business, your firm. You need to balance the time and money that you put into it against your dedication to family and faith—and, as we will see in the upcoming chapters, to fitness and fellowship. That balance will enhance, not deplete, your business dealings. Secure and content in the spectrum of life, you can be committed firmly to your firm.

Success requires commitment not only to the business and its functions but to the purpose behind it. We feel committed when we are pursuing something that we feel matters. When I launched BHW, I could have just started a therapy company that provided services. The greater task, however, was clear to me: I wanted to provide therapy in a way that would provide hope for people.

We must never forget the *why* of what we are doing. The comedian Michael Jr. once asked a member of his audience what he did for a living. "I'm a music director," the man said. When asked whether he could sing, he belted out a few lines of *Amazing Grace*. Michael Jr. then asked him to sing it again while thinking of what it meant to him, and the man's voice emanated such passion that he brought down the house. "When you know your *why*," Michael Jr. pointed out, "your *what* has more impact because you're walking in, or towards, your purpose."

The *why* of our lives, and of our businesses, has the power to bring light into dark places. When we operate out of a sense of purpose, we feel a greater desire to reach out into the world and offer something of enduring value. For me, what dispels the darkness is the power of hope. I wish to bring hope to families that often are broken and struggling.

BUILDING A FIRM THAT CARES

When you feel truly dedicated to whatever endeavor you are pursuing, you are far less likely to give up on your business pursuit, even in difficult circumstances. That firm commitment is the hallmark of businesspeople who care. Not only are they committed personally, but they surround themselves with colleagues of like minds—and they build a caring culture within the organization.

In my business life, I emphasize what I call the CARES philosophy, a model of five simple elements that are building blocks for success. It was at 4 a.m. one morning when I awoke with this inspiration and jotted it down on a napkin. Sometimes ideas crystallize during slumber.

The acronym CARES stands for compassionate, accountable, research-based, effective, and systems-oriented. It is a potent philosophy and an enlightening approach for building relationships and for building a business. It became the treatment model for patients at Behavioral Health Works.

I try to surround myself with compassionate people so that together we can build compassionate organizations. To find such people takes insight and discernment. One doesn't go to school to master in compassion. You cannot get a certificate. Still, it is an essential quality of those who will need to make the right decisions even in highly difficult circumstances.

I build accountability into the business structures. Not only does everyone need to be united in their vision for the company, but they also need to know how well they are advancing toward those goals. Every business needs key performance indicators, or KPIs. These are clear metrics that indicate advance-

The acronym CARES stands for compassionate, accountable, research-based, effective, and systems-oriented. It is a potent philosophy and an enlightening approach for building relationships and for building a business.

ment toward achieving objectives. They are the yardsticks of success. At a high level, they provide a snapshot of the overall performance of the organization. At lower levels, they reflect how departments or individuals are doing. At every level, they help to keep supervisors and employees on track to doing their very best.

A company providing quality products and services needs solid information based on sound research. The methodologies must be proven to be effective. Guesswork has no place. You cannot just have a hunch that what you are trying to do will work. You must be confident that it will work. A basis on research, then, is another critical element for entrepreneurs hoping to exhibit their very best.

Effectiveness is the goal, and the CARES model, as I have applied it, measures effectiveness in terms of long and sustainable progress. For example, BHW can provide autism treatment to get Johnny at age four or five to stop banging his head, but the concern extends well beyond that. BHW establishes goals for how the patient will still be benefiting when he or she is 18 or 20 and a working adult and how the patient will be interacting with family and peers through the years. Caring is more than an immediate fix. The philosophy of CARES takes a long-term perspective.

The systems approach of the model emphasizes that business functions must be performed as interrelated teamwork, not in isolation. At BHW, for example, the system consists of a variety of service providers and staff who work together toward a common purpose. The health of the organization depends on how well its parts work together, just as the behavioral health of little Johnny depends on how the various elements of his world work together. If treatment is to succeed, the caring must extend to the other stakeholders in his environment. The parents and grandparents, the teacher and coach, the neighbor—all of them potentially could be part of one system for treatment.

Whatever your enterprise, you should strive for a compassionate approach that emphasizes teamwork, holds one and all accountable for success, and that provides a proven and effective product. That is the kind of organization that will be committed to success.

The CARES philosophy is applicable to a wide range of businesses and organizations, and I have applied it in launching other endeavors besides BHW. Whatever your enterprise, you should strive for a compassionate approach that emphasizes teamwork, holds one and all accountable for success, and that provides a proven and effective product. That is the kind of organization that will be committed to success. That is the nature of a firm that cares.

THE THREE C'S

In evaluating employees for hiring or advancement purposes, I use three primary criteria that I call the three C's. Those criteria are character, chemistry, and competence—and it is in that order that I rate their importance. Together, they help to define an employee who will be committed to the firm.

I look first for the signs of good character: Does the employee have fundamental integrity and a cooperative, one-for-all spirit that is worthy of the organization? Is that employee willing, for example, to pick up a broom and sweep up a mess, no matter his or her title, without being compelled to do so? Does he or she exhibit a productive and dedicated work ethic, completing assignments efficiently and thoroughly? An employee of strong character will be honest, reliable, and trustworthy and will expect those traits in others.

How is the chemistry? Does he or she feel like a good fit for the culture? An organization makes the greatest progress toward its overall objectives when its people truly like one another, when they enjoy working together, when they collaborate eagerly and smoothly on the many tasks before them. When the goals are clear to all involved, the chemistry among employees tends to grow naturally, and that is why it is important to communicate the company strategy at all levels. Everybody should understand the *why* and his or her role in achieving it—even while sweeping up that mess.

Competence is undeniably important—but I would not rate it first. Competence requires context. A smart employee who is versed in the fundamentals is likely to acquire the required skills and expertise in due course—that is, if he or she has the other two qualities of the three C's. I have known workers who were highly competent at the outset but who needed to leave because they could not work well with teammates and did not share the vision. Their attitude was negative and poisonous. I have known others who clearly had a lot to learn—and who quickly learned a lot. They exhibited a spirit of enthusiasm and commitment that buoyed those around them, and with additional training they soon became exemplary employees.

EMPLOYING THE SCIENCE OF BEHAVIOR

My background as a behavioral health clinician has provided me with a wide variety of insights that I have been able to weave into my business practices. One psychology concept among many that I apply to the world of business is this: Behavior basically comes down to four functions, as discerned by the pioneers in behavioral psychology. Those functions determine how we each engage our environment and relate with those in the world around us.

In treating patients, clinicians look for the source of behaviors. What is driving a child, for example, to bite somebody or throw a tantrum? It may be to get attention, as if to say, "Look at me, I'm here, focus on me," and even "bad" attention can seem better than no attention. The child may be wanting access to something tangible, such as a favorite toy or enjoyable activity, and gets his way by screaming. The behavior may be an attempt to escape or avoid something—some situation or condition or requirement—rather than to get something. For example, the child may misbehave so she won't have to go outside to play with classmates. Perhaps the behavior has its roots in a sensory issue related to pleasure or pain—

the child cannot process the noise, lights, or other stimuli or has an unfulfilled physical need and reacts by lashing out.

Those four underlying functions of human behavior can be quite enlightening in understanding behaviors among employees as well as patients. The way that people act and interact on the job can be understood as attention-seeking behaviors, escape/avoidance behaviors, sensory/automatic reinforcing behaviors, and access-seeking behaviors. They want recognition; they want something to stop happening or something to start happening; or they want less pain and more pleasure. Sometimes the workplace conditions may not be conducive to productivity: Could the noise and light levels be better? Do the employees have sufficient break time?

Why, for example, is an employee submitting a resignation? Is it to access a better lifestyle because the pay is insufficient? If this is an employee of solid potential, the solution could be a raise or a better paying position with greater responsibilities. Why is an employee showing up late and not getting the job done on time, or at all? Could it be that he or she is trying to escape the prospect of failing at a task that seems too difficult by avoiding the task altogether? A simple solution might be better training and a realignment of responsibilities while the employee gains the necessary skills and confidence. And what is the real motivation behind what the employee communicates, whether the words or actions are positive or negative? Is it to gain attention? Is there a greater need for recognition?

The shaping of behavior is the key to success both in treating a child with autism and in improving the employment atmosphere. The goal is a more appropriate expression of the needs and wants that are common to all human beings. Good managers strive to recognize those needs and wants and to provide the channels for meeting them effectively. Otherwise, they are likely to surface in a less productive manner, threatening the chemistry and culture of the organization.

It starts with understanding. That is what leads to a breakthrough for the clinician and the patient, and that is what leads to a breakthrough for the employer and employee. Unacceptable behavior can be a symptom of something that is wrong systemically. Through understanding, we can learn what to do differently to encourage the desired results. "Use your words," parents sometimes tell children when they are acting cranky because they are tired or hungry. Some children do better by pointing to a picture—of a bed, for example, or a hamburger. They can alter the interaction to get what they need or want more effectively.

Employees certainly are not children and employers are not parents, but the principles of psychology apply wherever human beings interact. I have found that my professional background helps me greatly whether I am engaging with employees or with fellow entrepreneurs who are seeking to do more that matters. That understanding of human behavior is the basis of both the CARES philosophy and the three C's that I have found so valuable in building businesses.

Understanding begets compassion, and compassion should govern all our relationships. To do better in our world, we must commit our lives and our livelihoods to weeding out what is wrong and to nurturing what is right. What I have learned, I wish to share with others of like mind and heart.

An exercise for growth to serve a world in need:
FIRM COMMITMENT

For a balanced life, you need to give the proper perspective to whatever you are building—your practice, your business, your firm, your sports team, etc. The time and money that you commit to your firm must not sacrifice the importance of the other foundations.

Do you consistently spend more than 40 hours per week at work? If so, how can you bring down your time to an average of 40 hours per week?

_____

_____

_____

_____

_____

What are the top focus areas that your role requires of you? (e.g. management, strategy, forecasting, etc.)

_____

_____

_____

_____

_____

Track how you spend your time at work for one week, and graph the results on a pie chart. Determine whether you are spending your time wisely for the role that you are required to perform. Evaluate if you are effectively delegating: Are you performing tasks that should be completed by someone else, such as a colleague?

MONDAY	TUESDAY	WEDNESDAY	THURSDAY	FRIDAY
_____	_____	_____	_____	_____
_____	_____	_____	_____	_____
_____	_____	_____	_____	_____
_____	_____	_____	_____	_____
_____	_____	_____	_____	_____

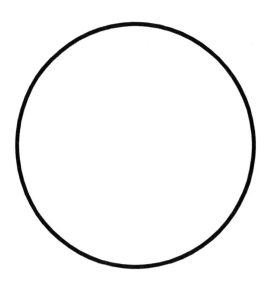

Develop a plan to self-manage your time more wisely. List your goals for 90 days and for 12 months as you move toward taking control of your work week.

_____

_____

_____

_____

CHAPTER 4

FITNESS TO SERVE

Living near some of the world's premier surfing spots, I admire those who challenge the waves. You would never guess the terror that I once felt of the water. When I was seven years old, I nearly drowned in a lake. My fear lingered for years. You might think it would have motivated me to learn to swim, but instead I avoided the water altogether. I would stand safely at the shore as the breakers came in, enviously watching the boogie boarders and surfers who seemed to have no fear of them.

Then when I was 18, I got a part-time job at an afterschool summer camp, and I had the responsibility of watching out for the welfare of preschoolers and kindergartners. I knew that my duties eventually would include being their lifeguard at the pool. How was

I to explain that I was afraid of the water? I knew that it was time to deal with this, and so I forced myself to learn to swim.

The fear soon dissipated. In its place, I felt a newfound confidence. The safety of these little ones had been entrusted to me, and I could not let them down. I could not let myself down. I committed myself to getting into tiptop shape so that I would be my best for them. Instead of hanging out with friends, I got to bed early each day so that I would be fresh on the job in the morning.

I wanted to be fit to serve in this new role, and I understood that I would need the tools to do so. At this point, refusing to learn to swim would be selfish and neglectful. I had to hone this skill so as not to put others in peril. I was doing the right thing. I was outside my shell, thinking of others, and I finally was acting in alignment with how God had wired me. I was striving to be my best so that I might serve a greater good. I was overcoming any obstacle that would stand in the way of helping others.

In the ensuing years, I became an enthusiastic surfer, and today I delight in the water. The water does not always delight in me, however. A few seasons ago, I nearly ripped off one of my toes while surfing. A severe infection set in that threatened to claim my right foot. I fully recovered, but the injury did keep me out of the water for a while and slowed down my ambitions to master the waves. I still enjoy paddle boarding, though, and I still look out wistfully to the sea as I did as a young man on the Italian Riviera.

I believe things happen for a reason—and so this setback has inspired me to turn my attention to earth and sky as well as sea. Namely, to golf and flying.

The former is a sport that I enjoy immensely as a time to share with colleagues and, lately, with my oldest son, Sekai. My loved ones can feel relatively confident that I will not be coming home with a severed toe. Golf is nonetheless a sport that is difficult to learn and requires discipline of mind and body. You must keep a good grip, but not overly tight. You must relax the big muscles so that they can do their work and send the ball in an ascendant arc. You need to know your clubs, reaching for just the right one to suit the occasion at hand. Be confident, keep your focus, but do not overdo it. Know when to let go. These are some of the lessons of the game that I am learning, and in many ways, they are like the lessons of life.

My wife supports my jaunts to the fairways, but she has been somewhat less sanguine about my aviation aspirations. In the spirit of marital oneness, I negotiated with Ami to win her consent. She finally agreed that I should continue pursuing my dream to get my private pilot's license, as well as experience the joys of skydiving and paragliding.

Learning to fly is like learning to surf and to golf, in that all three are difficult challenges that qualify as lifetime accomplishments. They require skill, discipline, perseverance, good judgment, and the confidence that is born of experience—much like the criteria for success in the business world. Seasoned surfers, for example, know that when a big wave pulls them down and under, they must look for the light and swim toward it. They do not waste energy trying to fight the cycles of the surf. Instead they understand it and go with the flow.

We must not let fear get in the way. Instead, we need to accept it, understand it, and let it motivate us. The journey from fear to faith teaches us to persevere and overcome—and knowing that we have overcome, we feel inspired to do more. I have spent time canyoning in Switzerland. When you are rappelling, you need to build a sense of confidence to step out. If you do not trust that rope, you might panic, and that's where the real danger lies. Entrepreneurs sometimes feel a similar sensation. That first big step can be frightening to anticipate. It's easier just to stay back in safe territory. Once you have built up a faith in your lifelines, however, you can swing out into greater adventures, over and over again.

Surfers, pilots and golfers all must quickly assess their circumstances to make smart decisions, but they understand and accept that they will always have more to learn. When you think you know it all, you cease to grow. The challenge for every one of us is to keep on learning about our world and its wonders so that we have ever more to offer our fellow mortals.

It is in that spirit that I aspire now to the sky. I intend to try skydiving soon, and I am hoping to paraglide with Ami's uncle at his farm in the Japanese countryside, where he is an avid practitioner of the sport. I already have tried paragliding once, in La Jolla, near San Diego. I discovered there how the birds must feel as they leverage the wind. From my lofty vantage point, I looked down upon one of my favorite golf courses, Torrey Pines, and outward to the wide Pacific. This was a God's eye view of sky, land, and sea. I felt as I did when I was a boy observing my neighborhood from my perch in the avocado tree. This was the world I knew.

I have not come close to mastery of golf, or surfing, or aviation, and that's okay. For me, the beauty is in the pursuit. What matters to me is that I am tackling something difficult to the best of my ability—and I strive to do so both in my vocation and in my avocations. I have learned that doing one's best requires living a balanced life. To be your best, you need to break away. You need to hold on to your dreams so that the workaday world does not smother you.

Only with that balance can you truly be fit to serve others. Nothing about leisure implies that you are lazy or less dedicated to making the most of life. In fact, it is quite the contrary: Living a balanced life gives you the opportunity to recharge and reach out.

As for me, I need the great outdoors, where my body and soul can rejuvenate. There I find the serenity that helps me to focus on what truly matters. My thoughts turn to the wisdom of the psalms: "Be still, and know that I am God."

I do recognize why family and colleagues sometimes worry about me. I hear their horror stories involving pilots of small planes and surfers and such. It is instinctive to want your loved ones to play it safe, and I wish to cause no one unnecessary anxieties. I just want them to understand, too. When I undertake these challenges, I feel more fully alive. I feel more fit to serve.

I think back to those childish days when I dreaded the water, and I see now that there is more than one way to drown. The fear was smothering me. That is what fear does. It was preventing me from being all that I could be for others. As I was embarking on adulthood,

> *I think back to those childish days when I dreaded the water, and I see now that there is more than one way to drown. The fear was smothering me.*

I was fortunate to have been thrust into a role that woke me up. I soon found out what I had been missing. I think back, also, upon what my parents and the other elders in my family have faced in their lifetimes. If they had succumbed to fear, I would not be here today. Through their faith in a future and their dedication to family, they overcame their fear.

This I know: We need to get back in the water. Unless we start swimming, we will be in no shape to pull others to safety. We have not been put here on earth to live selfishly for our own benefit. We are expected to pursue a healthy lifestyle that will honor others and honor God, doing our part to make the world better for others.

Some people fear that they will lose out on the fun that way, but to the contrary that is how we find joy. By filling others up, we fill ourselves up.

BEING OF SOUND BODY AND MIND

Most people think of fitness as keeping the body in good shape, but it is more than that. To be fit means that you must have good health and that you must have a healthy outlook. Fitness encompasses the body, mind, and soul. Effective servants strive to be fit physically, mentally, emotionally, and spiritually. All those forms of fitness work together to give you the wherewithal to serve others well. Physical exercise, for example, can go far toward enhancing your mental and emotional outlook.

> *To be fit means that you must have good health and that you must have a healthy outlook. Fitness encompasses the body, mind, and soul.*

As I have gotten into my middle years, I have come to recognize that my body is a temple. We need to treat our bodies as such and be good caretakers of the temple. The pursuit of success should never come at the expense of good health, because that's not success at all. Without physical fitness, we cannot serve to our capacity. We need to keep ourselves tuned up in all ways and to prime our bodies to serve others ever better.

Accomplishment requires stamina, and if you are not eating right and getting enough sleep and attending to your health, you will not be at your best. If your job involves physical activity, perhaps you are getting plenty of exercise. If your job is sedentary, however, you likely will need to put some extra effort into keeping yourself toned.

That doesn't necessarily mean that you are blowing it if you fail to go to the gym three times a week. Creative people can find endless ways to exercise. Any parent knows that keeping up with children can be physically demanding, for example, so think of those activities as a good workout. Instead of circling in frustration for a parking spot at the station, try leaving your car a few blocks away and walking briskly to meet the train. If you do that purposefully and allow time for it in your schedule, not only do you relieve the stress of parking but you also get the blood pumping at a healthful pace. Think of it not as wasted time but as an occasion for calisthenics.

Sometimes I think of my older self a decade or two from now. How would that older man advise this younger man to shape up while he still has time? There was a time when I celebrated my ability to work hard until late in the day and still show up early in the morning to do it all over. It is a perverse kind of thinking. It is self-defeating. When you are wearing yourself out, longer hours do not translate into more productivity. I have come to understand and appreciate how true that is. I would tell my younger self to focus first on fitness so that I can be around a long time to provide well for my family and to serve my community. Marriage and fatherhood have led me to think more holistically. That is a perspective that comes with maturity, and so I wonder what other insights and awakenings will come my way as I live and learn.

When you are wearing yourself out, longer hours do not translate into more productivity.

Stress comes to every life. How well you deal with it will depend, in large part, upon how well you are taking care of your temple. Physical fitness, with plenty of rest and good nutrition, is essential for effectively combating that stress. And when life feels overwhelming, it is wise to seek help. Many people walk among us suffering from post-traumatic stress from some nightmare of the past. Through treatment, they could find relief and freedom from the pain. Professional intervention could help them to cope and thrive—if they avail themselves of the opportunity to heal. Many do not. Fettered by their fears, they cannot live boldly.

ABILITY, AMBITION, ATTITUDE

On the wall near the stairwell at BHW, a spotlight illuminates a mural featuring these three words: *ability*, *ambition*, and *attitude*. These are the three essential A's of employee fitness and, by extension, of entrepreneurial fitness. They are the very ingredients of success.

> *In short, your ability defines what you are capable of doing; your ambition will determine what you end up doing; and your attitude will determine how well you do it.*

In short, your ability defines *what you are capable of doing*; your ambition will determine *what you end up doing*; and your attitude will determine *how well you do it*. To be fit requires all three. I can think of more than one athlete, for example, whose star faded because that final A of the trilogy was lacking. Some people with ample ability cannot muster the ambition to do much with it, and so they never realize their potential.

We are born with certain inclinations and talents. Those are God-given abilities. Some people are naturals at basketball, for example, and that is clear almost from the first time they pick up the ball. They are gifted with athletic prowess. Others are gifted with creativity, or with intellectual acuity. The range and combinations of human talents is boundless. Each of us has a unique set of physical, intellectual and spiritual gifts. What is important is to recognize those traits and make the most of them.

Ambition and the right attitude can propel us to victory, even when we have yet to develop our abilities to their potential. Many sports teams have done well even though no individual player is a star. Nonetheless, the team members play well together and are hungry for the win. Whether they are trailing or closing in on the title, they do what they need to do.

As an immigrant kid who had started life malnourished and in desperate circumstances, I long felt like the underdog, but I was blessed to have a family that encouraged me never to give in to an attitude of defeat. Instead, I was encouraged to close the gap. If I felt that I was behind, that meant I should run faster to catch up. The mindset was that I should do my very best with whatever I had.

I was blessed to have a family that encouraged me never to give in to an attitude of defeat. Instead, I was encouraged to close the gap.

I have seen businesspeople falling short of success because they are selling themselves short. They don't pursue their vision and persevere past the pain points. An attitude like that will prevent true success. They might have the talents and abilities. They might feel driven to succeed. They sink, however, in a pit of negativism and naysaying. When they face adversity, they fall back, feeling weak and dispirited. When they stumble, they are slow to regain their footing. Their attitude keeps them from doing the job well.

If you do not exercise your body, your muscles will weaken. You will grow flabby. If you do not exercise your gifts and your natural abilities, they too will fade. It's the adage of "use it or lose it." We must put our emphasis on the things that we do well. That is a lesson for businesses everywhere: Focus on what you do better than the competition. If you are an entrepreneur, ask yourself whether you truly are doing what you were cut out to do. If you are feeling worn out and are struggling with ambition, perhaps you have not found the right niche. If you do not like what you are doing, it is harder to do it well. Perhaps somebody else could bring more passion and profit to the task while you pursue your true calling.

When I am coaching others, I often ask this question: "Tell me about something that has always felt natural to you, something that has characterized you since you were a youngster." I hear such responses as: "I am a planner," or, "I am an organizer," or, "I am a leader." Then we compare that self-assessment with their pursuits in life. In other words, is what they are doing a good match for what they are wired to do? If so, that should nourish their ambition to do their best. If it is not a good match, that may be the root of the problem. When skills go unfulfilled, frustration and boredom set in. Ambition dies.

Even when the abilities and ambition are in place, something still may be missing. If you still feel held back and unable to reach the next threshold, it is time to look deeper: What attitudes are at work? Often, the dysfunctional attitude is rooted in fear: the fear of failing, the fear of risk, the fear of change. Fear has many faces. We hide from all manner of things. Ask yourself whether you are spending a lot of energy trying to cover up what should be out in the open—if not for the world to see, then at least for you to see.

Nothing gives me more pleasure than coaching others to help them realize their full potential. I have worked with talented people, for example, who have had challenges with substance abuse and helped them not only to stay clean but to maintain successful C-level jobs. One executive told me that the principles of coaching saved his marriage. I have seen people start out in tears and then unleash the power within them to find great success. They needed to discover themselves. Often what people need most is balance between their home lives and their work lives.

We must cast out what gets in the way. I believe that each of us has an appointed purpose and that we should waste no time in pursuing it. Through coaching, I can help people to understand themselves and feel motivated to be more and do more and go further. That way, they are better equipped to serve others.

To be our best is our calling in life, and by being our best we can serve at our best. You cannot help anybody until you can help yourself. When I was training to be a lifeguard, I had to prove that I was fit to serve before I could go on duty. After all, what good is a lifeguard who must be rescued himself? To be fit to serve starts with self-discovery, and together we can embark on that journey. It is an important step in taking care of business. It is an important step in serving a world in need.

An exercise for growth to serve a world in need:
FITNESS TO SERVE

To be in good shape, you must be physically fit, of course, but you must be mentally and emotionally fit as well. You need more than the ability to serve others: you need the ambition and a healthy attitude to follow through. Think of those as the three A's. Ability is what you are capable of doing. Ambition determines what you end up doing. Attitude determines how well you do it.

On a scale of 1 to 10, rate yourself on the three A's below, and reflect on why you score yourself that way.

Ability—*What am I capable of doing?*

1	2	3	4	5	6	7	8	9	10
Low				Average					Excel

Explain:

_____

_____

_____

_____

_____

_____

Ambition—*What am I doing with my abilities?*

1	2	3	4	5	6	7	8	9	10
Low				Average					Excel

Explain:

_____

_____

_____

_____

_____

_____

Attitude—*How well am I managing my abilities and ambitions?*

1	2	3	4	5	6	7	8	9	10
Low				Average					Excel

Explain:

_____

_____

_____

_____

_____

_____

Develop a plan to improve your three A's:

MY 90-DAY GOAL:

Ability

_____

_____

_____

Ambition

_____

_____

_____

Attitude

_____

_____

_____

MY 12-MONTH GOAL:

Ability

_____

_____

_____

Ambition

_____

_____

_____

Attitude

_____

_____

_____

CHAPTER 5

FELLOWSHIP AND SHARING

When I was 18 years old and itching to travel abroad, my father asked me: "Why in the world would you want to go to Europe? You can't even find your way around L.A. right now. Are you sure this is something you want to do?" He could see that I was still directionally challenged, but he did not see that I was aching to experience the world. I have long understood the importance of seeking counsel from loved ones and trusted associates. You should care to hear from those who care about you. The decision, however, is not theirs. We each must make our own choices.

I know that my father, despite his misgivings, was proud of me nonetheless. His protective spirit—the same one that motivated him to lead his family out of Cambodia—simply wanted the best for me. He wanted me to avoid the pains and troubles that come from interacting in this world. He knew I had so much more to learn. The irony is that the learning comes from those interactions. Some are pleasant, and some are not, but through it all we grow.

> *He wanted me to avoid the pains and troubles that come from interacting in this world. He knew I had so much more to learn. The irony is that the learning comes from those interactions. Some are pleasant, and some are not, but through it all we grow.*

I did get on that plane to Europe. It was my first flight since I was a baby. The trip changed me. I went to the University of Granada for a month or two to study Spanish and then backpacked across the continent. With my eyes open wide, I experienced the cultures of more than a dozen countries. I met and learned from people my own age and from others who had seen a bit more of life. I observed that a welcoming smile and the word for *hello* goes a long way in any language.

This was a season of discovery, a time of both introspection and outreach. It amounted to far more than a Spanish lesson that I could check off for my language requirement. In those early days of my college career, I already had been experiencing new worlds that were opening to me. This was a euphoric time of exciting ideas and perspectives that I never had encountered. Now, beyond the confines of the classroom, I was learning even more about myself and about others. I discovered that people with whom you have spent only a few days can have a profound impact on you. A moment shared—whether it is one of laughter or tears, of buoyant chatter or gentle silence—can reverberate for a lifetime. We must get to know our fellow travelers.

Such is fellowship. It is not simply some party mentality. Fundamentally, I am an introvert. I recharge in solitude, which gives me boundless energy to take on the world. I could play alone, but my heart's desire is to be of service to others in meaningful relationships. Fellowship is about making those contacts.

It is much more, however, than exchanging business cards in some sterile gesture of networking. In the spirit of fellowship, we do not look for what we can get out of our relationships but rather for how we can grow together and make life better for one another. We should commune with others, through the laughter and the tears, and together pursue what really matters. That's what friends do.

When you are humble enough to reach out to others to tap into their knowledge and experiences, you begin to flourish. Each of us has a piece of the puzzle of life. We each have different skills and interests and aptitudes, and in fellowship we can assemble our strengths into a beautiful and powerful whole. As we come together to share and collaborate, we grow stronger as a people, and we grow stronger as individuals. We need one another.[1]

---

1   "Be the Entrepreneur of Your Life—Women Business Owners Share How," *Inc.* October 24, 2017, https://www.inc.com/genesis/be-the-entrepreneur-of-your-life.html.

During the Great Depression, researchers at Harvard University began tracking the lives of hundreds of men in a long-term study[2] seeking to determine how their lives would turn out and why. Each year starting in 1938, the study asked the subjects, from their youth into their old age, to report on their lives, their careers, and the state of their physical and mental health. The study group comprised Harvard sophomores and, later, young men from inner-city Boston. Over the decades, the researchers collected voluminous data based on interviews, questionnaires, and medical records. Some of the subjects attained success, and others struggled. After analyzing the mountain of information, the researchers have identified the most important factor in determining the men's happiness and health. It wasn't wealth and fame. It wasn't their social class or their level of intelligence. It was the quality of their relationships. Those who flourished and stayed the healthiest, both mentally and physically, tended to have strong social ties with family, friends, and the community.

"No man is an island, entire of itself," wrote the poet and cleric John Donne. "Any man's death diminishes me, because I am involved in mankind, and therefore never send to know for whom the bell tolls; it tolls for thee." It's a big world, and we cannot go it alone. We must make time enough to share. Fellowship is the culmination of the five F's.

THE FELLOWSHIP OF FAMILY

I was in my early 20s when I visited the land where I was born. During my first year out of college, I helped to lead a group of high

---

2   Liz Mineo, "Good genes are nice, but joy is better," *Harvard Gazette*, April 11, 2017, https://news.harvard.edu/gazette/story/2017/04/over-nearly-80-years-harvard-study-has-been-showing-how-to-live-a-healthy-and-happy-life/.

school students on a church mission trip. I assisted in supervising a dozen or so boys. We spent two weeks in Thailand working with orphans and helping villagers to develop a fish farm so that young people had options other than migrating to the cities by the age of 12 and falling victim to human traffickers. For days, we dug pits to build the fish farm. When we had completed our task, I arranged a personal side trip across the border into my homeland.

Cambodia was a place unlike any that I had ever known. It didn't resemble anything that I had seen from the avocado tree. It was worlds away from our little trailer in the desert. Much of this land was extraordinary. I had a chance to see the countryside and the beaches and the ruins of a magnificent temple in the jungle. I saw the poverty, too, and the plight of so many Cambodian people.

In Phnom Penh, I visited the humble home of my father's mother—my other grandmother who had been unable to join the family as we fled the Khmer Rouge when I was a newborn. Those horrific times splintered many families. She had never had the opportunity to hold her little grandbaby, or even see me, and now finally we embraced. I felt joy in meeting her, as well as in meeting an assortment of aunts and distant cousins who came to see their American relative from another era, another world.

As I tried to keep track of who was who, I began to feel overwhelmed. This wave of intense emotion was much different from what I had experienced while backpacking in Europe just a few years earlier. Something moved within me: This was my family, too, and this land was the wellspring of my heritage. These were my people, and this easily could have been my life. As refugees, we had struggled. As new immigrants, we had faced endless uncertainties. I recognized that those good people there in the room with me had faced their own struggles and uncertainties during difficult years. All of us had been shaped by our experiences and by those who had come into our lives. Truly, I had been fortunate.

Fellowship begins at home, where we foster our earliest relationships. We each must ask ourselves how we will be remembered, and the answer largely will be determined by what we have shared with others throughout our lives. Our legacy is more than monetary. We bestow, too, a big part of our hearts and souls. As we journey together, we can shape and sharpen one another. A caring mentor or a good friend can make the difference that endures for generations. A dedicated and loving parent can engender attitudes that will serve their children better than a multimillion dollar inheritance. It is a power beyond the portfolio.

> *Fellowship begins at home, where we foster our earliest relationships. We each must ask ourselves how we will be remembered, and the answer largely will be determined by what we have shared with others throughout our lives.*

I am grateful to have been welcomed warmly into my grandmother's home in Cambodia—and I never will forget something I saw there. It was a series of framed photographs hanging from a rope. She displayed them that way because they were impossible to attach to the concrete walls. The photos were years old, and I saw among them my own face—my second-grade picture, my third-grade picture. Hanging from that rope were the images of her loved ones far away, some of whom she had never seen. She had been delighted to receive them—and someone had been delighted to send them.

"FORWARD" THINKING

A sense of fellowship engendered within the family soon will spread to the community. A caring spirit reaches outward. As we will see in the next section, the spirit of giving back to one's fellow man is an important element of business success, as well as a foundation for a balanced life. The principle of "paying it forward" embodies the deep concern for others that should be the hallmark of every successful entrepreneur.

> *The spirit of giving back to one's fellow man is an important element of business success, as well as a foundation for a balanced life.*

To whom much is given, much is expected. Once we recognize the blessings that have come our way, it becomes our duty to sow that good fortune in the lives of those around us. Our world has many needs. If someone does you a good turn, you may wish to find a way to pay that person back. That is a noble instinct, of course, but you do not need to think of a good deed as a debt that you personally owe to the giver. You can think of it as an inspiration to "pay it forward" instead of paying it back.

You can make it your mission to contribute something to society of equal or greater value that will benefit others for years to come. Your gift is all the more meaningful when it comes from an appreciative and joyful heart. When you begin to focus on others, your energy can seem boundless.

Before I got married, my brother arranged a bachelor's trip with several friends to hike the Half Dome at Yosemite National Park and go white-water rafting. We were all in reasonably good shape and healthy, but I can't say that we were well prepared for the rigors of our adventure. We started out by charging up the mountain like a bunch of happy lunatics. We soon learned the importance of stretching and prepping our muscles so that they would not cramp up. And each of us at times truly needed the help of our fellow man. At one point, I found myself lending a shoulder to nudge my brother up the incline—and he is nearly twice my size.

Even though I, too, need a helping hand from our friends, I noticed this: I felt charged with energy so long as I was focused on being the helper. It was only when I turned my attention back to myself, thinking about my own weary legs and my own thirst, that I felt weary and grew slower. My strength came from looking out for the needs of the others. I am sure each of us experienced something similar.

The lesson is clear: When we have one another's back, we can climb to ever greater heights. We can do far more in fellowship than we would ever accomplish alone.

An exercise for growth to serve a world in need:
FELLOWSHIP AND SHARING

When we are in fellowship with others, we are developing the friendships and the contacts that we need for a meaningful life. We must develop strong relationships and share our experiences so that together we can pursue what really matters. Along the way, we are building our legacy.

List the people, or the groups, with whom you hang out during the course of a month for fun and leisure. Do you give yourself enough time to relax with friends?

_____

_____

_____

_____

_____

_____

From whom do you receive mentorship or discipleship at least once a month? Is this someone who possesses the wisdom, either professional or personal, to help you to pursue a balanced life?

_____

_____

_____

_____

_____

_____

Whom do you mentor at least once a month? This might be an apprentice, or your successor, or someone to whom you are "giving back" as you further your mission.

_____

_____

_____

_____

_____

_____

DEVELOP AN ACTION PLAN FOR FELLOWSHIP:

Which relationships will I develop within 90 days? Why do I want to nurture them?

_____

_____

_____

_____

Which relationships will I develop in the next year? Why do I want to nurture them?

_____

_____

_____

_____

Whom will I mentor during those periods? Who will mentor me?

_____

_____

_____

_____

How will the relationship benefit each of us?

_____

_____

_____

_____

PRINCIPLES OF BUSINESS SUCCESS

The Five Principles

CHAPTER 6: PASSION WITHIN

CHAPTER 7: PURPOSE TO PURSUE

CHAPTER 8: PLAN OF ACTION

CHAPTER 9: PRIME TIME

CHAPTER 10: PAYING IT FORWARD

CHAPTER 6

PASSION WITHIN

Of this, I was certain: Money mattered. As I headed off to college, the day after that frightful night when I was accosted at gunpoint in Long Beach, I had no doubt that money meant something better for me and my family—and so I set out in pursuit of it. I wanted the best return on investment that education could buy.

College would be my way out, and my way up. It would be my route to a high-paying job. This was more than a dream. I felt it was my duty to my family, and so I was highly disciplined in my approach to the collegiate life. I would schedule 8 o'clock classes and get to them on time, after making my bed, while other kids were staying up late to play video games and going out for breakfast burritos at 4 a.m.

I was determined to do whatever it would take to become my own version of a huge success. I wanted the "good life" and all that I imagined it could bring. To me at the time, that meant I had to make a lot of money. Frankly, I had little knowledge of myself. I didn't have a grasp on what truly would make Rob Douk happy. I had little understanding of the passion that lay within me and that ultimately would drive my life.

> *I wanted the "good life" and all that I imagined it could bring. To me at the time, that meant I had to make a lot of money. Frankly, I had little knowledge of myself.*

To lead a successful life, or run a successful enterprise, you need to understand how you are wired and what motivates you. When you are true to yourself, you will feel flushed with ambition to do your best and to be your best. "Passion" is the first of the five principles of business success.

A TIME OF AWAKENINGS

College came as a cultural shock on a variety of fronts. Coming from a rough background, I was not accustomed to looking people in the eye with a smile and a friendly hello. I had left a high school where the gangster culture was idolized. Even young people who were not part of that scene nonetheless dressed and acted the part. To be open and transparent with others was not cool. In that culture, a guarded attitude was considered smart. You were weak if you revealed too much about yourself.

Though I had been conditioned to act circumspect among my peers, my heart felt otherwise—and I soon met others in college who were a much better match for my makeup. I was meeting people from the far reaches of California and the far reaches of the nation, converging in that dormitory setting, and the experience confirmed by belief that most people tend to be warm and outgoing by nature. They do not want to hide behind a façade. They are not suspicious of a friendly greeting.

It didn't take long before Ami caught my eye—in fact, we met on campus during the first day of freshman orientation. I spotted her across the room at a welcoming event. She was beautiful. I noticed that right away. And then I felt drawn to her illuminating smile. She projected a gentle, childlike innocence. I got the immediate impression of a spirit that was down to earth and grounded. She wore jeans and a T-shirt that sported the name of a band, the Supertones, which I later learned was a Christian ska group.

A little later, while I was chatting with other freshmen, I turned to see that huge smile approaching me. Now, where I came from, that would clearly have meant that she was interested in me. And she was, although not in the way that I at first imagined. She was interested in everyone in the room. She wanted to get to know all her new friends in the dorms. We still joke about my initial misinterpretation of her intentions, although we tell the story in somewhat different ways.

The cultural shock of college, for the most part, was a good one. I quickly loosened up and felt free and safe about being my real self around others—

The cultural shock of college, for the most part, was a good one. I quickly loosened up and felt free and safe about being my real self around others— although every day I was learning more about who that was.

although every day I was learning more about who that was. This was a time of personal and social growth, as it is for many young people at that age. I explored new interests, including different styles of music and the arts, that had been lying dormant within me. My senses came alive. Anything seemed possible then, and I wanted to find out all that I could about this world. At every turn, it seemed, I was on the verge of something exciting. To this day, I miss that time, those days of awakening when everything was bright and new.

I even loved the dormitory life, as did Ami and some of my other friends, to the point where we struck a deal with the college so that we could remain residents in the dorms for a second year. We became event coordinators. We set up social events for the students in the dorms, and that way we got to stay. I enjoyed the prospect of meeting and hanging out with hundreds of incoming freshmen, each excited about this new adventure. I thrived on the challenge of building a strong culture among the students. I was truly a social being, and I could see that Ami was much like me.

I was falling in love with Ami, and I soon learned that she was a package deal. She shared with me her Christian faith, and as the good word began to permeate my heart, I found that I also was falling in love with Jesus. In loving him, I loved even more this young woman in whom he resided. My circle of friends increasingly included the faith community. Ami and I got involved in the New Song Church and The Edge campus ministry. At the same time, I was beginning to live a frat house lifestyle that threatened to distract me from my newfound faith. At a time when I was searching spiritually, Ami was the perfect person to come into my life.

Ami's parents had emigrated to Southern California from Japan. They had long been intrigued with the prospect of coming to America. In fact, they named their two girls Ami and Rika—together,

Ami-Rika—in tribute to their newfound home. Ami's mother had become a Christian, as did Ami and Rika when they were in their early teens. When I met Ami, her parents were getting a divorce. That was a tough time for her, and I became, in a way, her comedian who kept her smiling. We were together constantly, studying, laughing, hanging out. Others recognized that we were a couple, even before we did.

GETTING BACK IN TOUCH

I know now that I have two primary passions—for business, and for helping people—and during my undergraduate years, I was pushing aside the significance of the latter. The focus of my studies was economics, in keeping with my desire to make a lot of money. The school did not yet offer a business degree. I interned at major financial firms, including UBS Financial Services, PaineWebber, and Merrill Lynch. I was determined to take that path, even though I was enjoying some of my elective classes much more, particularly psychology.

It wasn't as if I was oblivious to my desire to help others. In my high school yearbook, I had written that I wanted to "change the world through the lens of a pediatrician helping children live healthy lives." Early on, I knew that I had a love for healing and working with children. In high school, I had been volunteering in an after-school program for kids and saw the great potential to have a lasting impact. I imagined a career working with young people in a clinical setting. In college, however, I disregarded that interest. I felt it was my mission to capitalize quickly on a college education. Pre-med would take too long.

Eventually, I double majored in international studies and sociology. I would have loved to have majored in psychology, and I was jealous of the classes that Ami got to take. I gained clarity through knowing her, but nothing could steer me off the course that I had appointed for myself. I held fast to my financial track. I valued discipline, order and persistence. I was proud of my focus and my ability to delay gratification. I had promises to keep.

Nonetheless, I chose those two broad majors that reflect a love for people and for cultures. I studied abroad. Later, when I pursued my business degree, it would be a "global executive" MBA, which required me to travel. All along, I was exhibiting an inner passion to reach out to the world. And all along, I was showing my dedication to the business world and my respect for entrepreneurs, who have the power to make money and to use it for our common good.

> *I do not mean to imply in any way that money is a bad thing or that a love for business somehow suggests a lack of social sensitivity. It's very much the opposite.*

I do not mean to imply in any way that money is a bad thing or that a love for business somehow suggests a lack of social sensitivity. It's very much the opposite. I have extensive business experience, and I know how to make money. I'm wired that way, just as I'm wired to help people. In college, I became enamored of life's possibilities—and money opens the door to those possibilities. The best businesses thrive and make money because they know how to serve others well. That is why I am focusing today on helping the "socialpreneurs" among us to build their businesses for the benefit of all. It's a way of bringing together my two passions.

Yes, the pursuit of money mattered to me immensely in my college years, but if I had looked deeper into my heart I would have understand that it mattered because it could help people, and people were my passion. I wanted to be part of their journeys and their stories and to somehow make their lives better. I was intrigued by why people do what they do, and I felt driven to understand them.

For the time being, however, that passion would wait. I had another agenda. I wanted to take control of my life and my path to success, so I headed out to make my mark on the world. It would be a few years before I hit a wall of frustration that drove me back to the classroom. I had to face the emptiness and reach the point where I could ask God to fill me up.

An exercise for growth to serve a world in need:
PASSION WITHIN

Each of us has a story to tell, whether we know it or not, and the theme of that story is likely to reflect a deeply rooted passion—and perhaps one that still is waiting to be expressed. In this exercise, let's explore the milestones in your life journey and identify what has influenced you to make you what you are.

STEP 1: WHAT DO YOU KNOW ABOUT YOURSELF?

Create a timeline. Start from your birth and chart out all of the major life events that led to where you are now.

Write down what you know about your strengths and interests. For example: What was your favorite subject in elementary school? What were your favorite hobbies? What have you observed about yourself that comes naturally to you?

List the few pursuits that interest you so much that you are willing to stay up late and lose sleep?

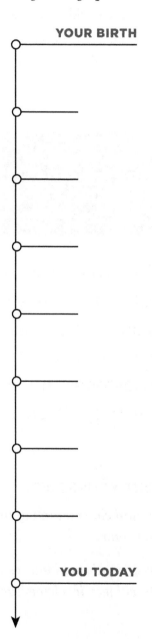

YOUR BIRTH

YOU TODAY

STEP 2: WHAT DO OTHERS KNOW ABOUT YOU?

Interview three people who know you well and ask them the following questions:

What am I passionate about?

_____

_____

_____

_____

What are three things that I do well and that seem to come naturally to me?

_____

_____

_____

_____

What experiences do you believe have shaped me and influenced my passions?

_____

_____

_____

_____

If I didn't have to work for money, what do you think I would be doing?

_____

_____

_____

_____

STEP 3: IDENTIFYING THE THEMES

Now, analyze your timeline, your self-assessment, and the assessment of others from your interviews. List any trends that you observe. For example, does your timeline suggest you have been a natural leader—perhaps as the captain of your high school basketball team, all the way to your current role in business?

_____

_____

_____

_____

_____

_____

_____

STEP 4: COMPLETE THE FOLLOWING STATEMENT WITH YOUR NEWFOUND KNOWLEDGE:

"I have been passionate about _____ (one word or phrase) since _____ (year, or age), according to _____ (identify the source of that insight).

Example: "I have been passionate about <u>leadership</u> since <u>age 5</u>, according to <u>my parents</u>."

CHAPTER 7

PURPOSE TO PURSUE

What could possibly be wrong? I had done what I set out to do. I had taken all the right classes and secured the best internships and graduated with a great grade point average, and now I was working for a major insurance company making more money right out of college than any of my friends. Shouldn't I be happy? Wasn't this the American dream that I had been driving so hard to experience?

The bosses seemed to like me. I was hitting my numbers. I was making my metrics. I was showing every sign of dedication, working after hours to demonstrate for all to see that I was a rising star. Already I had received one promotion. And now my supervisors were shaking my hand once again, telling me I was great, offering me another promotion. I smiled, went home, and wrote my resignation letter.

Perhaps I was stubborn, perhaps I was immature, but until then I had not acknowledged that I wasn't cut out for such a cutthroat environment—or at least that is how the atmosphere of an insurance company felt to me at the time. I did not feel that I was helping anyone or anything other than the firm. It was a living, but to call it a "good" living is to equate goodness with gain. I knew I was born for more than that. Corporate insurance is, of course, an important industry that undoubtedly helps others. It is a worthwhile pursuit, but it didn't do much for my self-worth. Every day I struggled with the feeling that there must be more to life than this. I knew that I was a man designed to reach out, but I was pulling in.

> *I did not feel that I was helping anyone or anything other than the firm. It was a living, but to call it a "good" living is to equate goodness with gain.*

Years later, sitting in my spacious office in the headquarters of my own company, I could look out the window and see that building where I first started. In my mind's eye, I could see a sharply dressed young man who takes the elevator down to the lobby at lunch time and emerges into the sunlight. He crosses the street to the shopping center, where he sits in the Barnes & Noble café, eats the ham sandwich that his father makes for him daily, sips his apple juice, and reads. He flips through books that he has found in the store's self-improvement section—books such as *What Color is Your Parachute?* by Richard Nelson Bolles. The young man knows that he needs to better understand what makes him tick. He needs to find himself. Every workday he has been driving himself hard for the first four hours. By lunchtime, he feels deflated, and so he comes here in search of answers.

That was me, years ago when I was the new graduate out to conquer the world but feeling more like the world was conquering him. As I began to read those books, I spent a lot of time in search of the authentic me. Would the real Rob Douk please stand up? Sometimes I would go to lunch with my colleagues, but mostly I spent that hour alone in my time of self-discovery. It was a lonely interlude in my life, but once again I felt driven by a determination. If my purpose was not simply to make a lot of money, then what was expected of me?

> *As I began to read those books, I spent a lot of time in search of the authentic me. Would the real Rob Douk please stand up?*

I was aware by then that my passion was not just the world of business. I needed somehow to make it my business to help others in a way that would feel meaningful to me. Now that I knew my passion, my problem was that I was failing to exercise it. In fact, I had been actively trying to ignore it. Let me be clear: That never works. You must put a purpose to your passion. You must pursue a vocation that reflects who you truly are. Discovering and pursuing your purpose in life is the second principle of business success.

FAREWELL, MY ANGEL

With our college graduation approaching, Ami and I both had known that it was time to say goodbye. Together we decided that we each should focus on our relationship with God. This was an excruciatingly hard decision. Ami was my angel. "God, if I am to let her go," I told him, "I will just forever think of her as the angel you sent to me during my college years, when you saved me." We didn't try to tell each other that we would be getting back together soon or even someday.

I know now that this was a crucial juncture. I would soon be wrestling with some deep questions. If Ami had still been in my life, I am not sure that I ever would have resolved those issues adequately. I needed to endure those lonely days as I struggled to find out what God wanted me to do in life. I was still a child on my Christian walk, and Ami had been with me every step. I felt as if my faith had become contingent upon her encouragement. I needed to find my own way, and so did she. We had become too comfortable together, to the point that we were at risk of stifling each other's growth. God needed our full and undistracted attention.

> If Ami had still been in my life, I am not sure that I ever would have resolved those issues adequately.

Ami and I didn't get back together until I had discovered that money wasn't everything and I had made the decision to return to graduate school. Money was a means, not an end. I finally had clearly recognized that my passion was to help people, particularly children. Among the books that I had been reading was *The Purpose Driven Life* by Rick Warren, which led me to ponder how God wanted to shape my future. I was learning to discern his voice. I wanted a life based on passion, not profits. I no longer cared about promotions and big raises. I wanted only to know my calling.

When Ami learned of my soul-searching, she found me to be more attractive than ever. We reunited but decided to wait several years before marriage and, in the meantime, to live purely in our relationship with each other and with God. I think of our two years apart as our time in the desert, when we each were fine-tuning our character and searching for God's will. We did not marry until 2006, when we were 27 years old. The two became one.

IN TOUCH WITH THE HEART

I had been doing it all wrong. I came to see that. I recognized that the God who had designed me and who had given me certain gifts was watching to see just how I would use them—and I knew that I would not be using them well by simply hanging in there and hammering away at a job that did not fit me. Even though I was flying high, something needed to bring me down, and ironically it was my promotion that did it. If I had stubbornly held on to that job, I might have been promoted again and again to the point of despair—and I was close enough to that already.

Once again, my sense of discipline served me well. Sometimes young people, in the excitement of a new job, go out to buy expensive new cars and get themselves deeply into debt. They fall into a financial trap and cannot say, "I don't want to do this anymore." At least I had kept my options open, and at least I knew that something was wrong. That's the first step toward doing something about it.

This crucial period of self-examination allowed me to recognize the misalignment

> *Sometimes young people, in the excitement of a new job, go out to buy expensive new cars and get themselves deeply into debt. They fall into a financial trap and cannot say, "I don't want to do this anymore."*

between what I was doing and what was in my heart. It did not matter that I was doing well by the company's standards. I needed to be doing well by my own standards, and my own standards needed to be aligned with the standards of my maker and designer. My thoughts increasingly turned to the big picture. Where had I been, and where was I heading?

As I drifted off to sleep at night, I would see images from the past. I saw myself as a frightened young man held at gunpoint late at night by a stranger demanding to know who he was. *Who are you? Who ARE you?* I thought I knew then. I knew nothing. I saw the same young man sitting with his backpack at the ocean's edge, asking that same question as he marveled at the power of the one who had set the waves in motion. Who was God, and who was I? I saw myself holding a dear friend in my arms, praying that he would not die that way. I saw a cross beaming from a hillside, and then in its place I saw a huge smile beaming at me from across a room. It grew closer and almost blindingly bright until suddenly it receded from me and seemed to blink out. Time and again, I had thought I finally understood, but those were merely clues to a great mystery. I had remained a frightened young man who did not know who he was.

And I imagined other scenes from the past during those lonely days. Now I saw another young man. He was casting nets to the tide and secretly selling fish for the money he would need to bribe the enemy so that he and his family might escape from hell. He knew that money mattered, but this young man had no doubt as to why. I saw that same man laughing with his children as they frolicked in their first snowfall, catching the flakes on their tongues. I saw, too, a young woman huddled on the scarred earth, her arms wrapped around her newborn baby. And there she was again, out in the yard now with her loved ones, her arms wrapped tightly around another newborn baby in another land of so much promise and so many wonders. My family had struggled in this new land, but we had come so far. We had been given so much. How could I give back?

Whatever I did, I knew that it would be worthy only if I put God first. I would not be happy without the help of the one who knew what I needed to make me happy. "Show me what you want me to do," I prayed, "and whatever it is, I will do my best for you." I had no doubt that he would answer that prayer, and I did not need to wait for some epiphany of insight. I could see that God had been showing me all along, and he had been continuously beckoning to me. I just needed to answer his call. I needed to give up control to him. It was with joy that I wrote that letter of resignation. Even with no idea what I would do next, I felt a sense of confidence. I knew that it would be good.

FINDING THE FOCUS

So now what? I still felt that I needed to be making good money, and so after resigning from that corporate insurance sales job, I figured my next move logically would be to get an MBA degree because, after all, business was my passion, too, and it would be the means by which I could help people. The first step would be the graduate management admission test, or GMAT, and so I began to study. It was the same old me, focusing intensely, planning and organizing, determined to make it. I felt as I did when I was getting up to make those 8 o'clock classes.

Something still was missing. I had not defined "helping people." I still had no clear picture of my purpose. How would I put that passion into action? What would be its manifestation? I began to ask questions of everyone who knew me well, including my parents, relatives, and friends. *What am I good at? What do you see me doing for a career? When I was a kid, what seemed to come naturally for me?* The questions had a common theme: What did they see as my passion and my purpose in life? I was hoping to tap into their insights and wisdom. I figured that they could help me to identify the appropriate endeavor that I could put into a business setting. They might see things about me that I could not see myself.

> *The questions had a common theme: What did they see as my passion and my purpose in life? I was hoping to tap into their insights and wisdom.*

A particularly helpful suggestion came from my Aunt Sophea as we sat at my mother's kitchen table. "You are really good with people," she told me, "and you are a good listener. I've always seen how much you like to help people." She paused, and then turned to look into my eyes: "Dom, you know, I could see you being a psychologist."

Though I had enjoyed studying psychology, I never had seriously considered it as a career path. Her suggestion came as a surprise. But the seed was planted. Others were telling me similar things about myself. That very evening, as I was doing some career research online, I chanced upon an article in U.S. News & World Report. Within the next several years, the article said, there would be a shortage of men working as psychologists in the United States because so many of them who had taken up the profession as baby boomers soon would be retiring.

I became fascinated at the prospect of becoming a psychologist. I had identified a potential purpose that I felt eager to explore. I didn't know what psychologists did, but I was convinced that the profession would be a good fit for me and a worthy goal. Now I just needed to figure out how to go about realizing that objective. I needed a plan of action.

ALL PART OF THE PLAN

When you finally recognize and nurture a passion, it evolves into a purpose. It becomes a vocation that is satisfying to the soul. Every one of us needs to reflect on the timeline of life. Think about what you have done, what you have accomplished, and how it contributed toward building something greater. You must first come to understand yourself. You need to truly know who you are and what drives you. Otherwise, life feels aimless.

When you finally recognize and nurture a passion, it evolves into a purpose. It becomes a vocation that is satisfying to the soul.

Stepping out on faith is not necessarily easy. It can feel daunting to take any kind of risk, even when you are finally getting your big chance, and that is why would-be entrepreneurs often hesitate to put a purpose to their passions. When you have faith in the future, as we explored in Chapter 1, you can conquer that fear. You feel free to move forward without the shackles of doubt. No way will you be spending a lifetime languishing in excuses and indecision.

I do not regret the moneymaking focus of my undergraduate years, nor my early experience in the financial field. I gained valuable skills and perspectives. Nor do I regret the frustrations that I faced then, because they led me to a period of serious soul-searching. As a result, I have a greater empathy today as a business coach. I know what it feels like. I've been there. It was all part of a bigger plan that helped to prepare me to fulfill a purpose. It was all part of the foundation upon which dreams can be built.

An exercise for growth to serve a world in need:
PURPOSE TO PURSUE

Why do so many people dip a toe into the pool and shiver as they slowly wade in? Pools are there for a purpose—namely, so you can have fun—so why not jump in cannon ball style! You can live a cannon ball type of life, as well, but you first need to put a purpose to your passion. Living a purposeful life means you know what you are doing. You don't want to dive into the shallow end, and you must learn to swim before making that big splash.

A survey asked 95-year-olds what they would have done differently in life. Their responses can be summed up with three words: ripples, reflection, and risk. Think of them as the three R's for a purposeful life. As you identify your life goals, put them on a timeline so that you can monitor your progress toward reaching them. Then find an accountability partner to give you regular support and feedback as you pursue those three R's.

RIPPLES

Your time is precious, so spend it on the pursuits that will outlive you to become your legacy. You can send ripples into the generations to come, which will remember you by your initiatives and innovations.

Complete this sentence: *"I will dedicate my working hours to* _____ *(name of company or activity), and the ripple impact that I will leave will be:*

_____

_____."*

Let me share with you how I completed that sentence on three occasions when I was venturing into new endeavors. Each time, I was establishing a purpose for my passion for helping others:

"I will dedicate my working hours to Behavioral Health Works, and the ripple impact that I will leave will be to help individuals with autism improve their quality of life and provide hope to families. I will leave a legacy of generosity as I share my time in clinical experiences with young therapists to encourage them to become ambassadors of hope for families in need."

"I will dedicate my working hours to Hope Out Loud, and the ripple impact that I will leave will be providing clean water to over 15,000 people by 2020, providing behavioral treatment to over 5,000 families in developing countries by 2020, and providing alternative work skills to 1,000 survivors of human trafficking by 2020."

"I will dedicate my working hours to Douk & Company, and the ripple impact I will leave will be empowering other entrepreneurs and executives to create extraordinary companies that benefit society.

REFLECTION

After each work day, take some time to reflect on the desires of your heart that already are yours. Show your appreciation for your loved ones; set aside the distractions of technology and "enjoy more sunsets" with them.

Here is an example of a promise you might make to yourself:

> "I will dedicate my nonworking time to reflect more on my blessings. Instead of spending so many hours on social media or answering work emails, I instead will devote that time to activities with my wife and children. I will devote Sundays to family time, closing out each weekend with a family dinner."

_____

_____

_____

_____

_____

_____

RISK

If you are reluctant to try new things for fear of failure, you will lose out on a lot of life's adventures. Try stepping out of your comfort zone and taking a few risks. Continuously challenge yourself intellectually, physically, emotionally and culturally. To increase your chances of success, hold yourself accountable by setting goals.

Here are some examples of goals that I have set for myself, fully aware of the risk that I might fall short:

"I will challenge myself intellectually by reading at least one new book each quarter and by obtaining my pilot's license within a year. I will challenge myself physically to eat healthful meals and to work out three times a week. I will challenge myself culturally by traveling to someplace new to me at least once a year for vacation or on a mission trip."

_____

_____

_____

_____

_____

_____

CHAPTER 8

PLAN OF ACTION

As I set out to become a psychologist, I knew one thing, and that was that I didn't know much at all. That was my greatest strength at the time. Far worse than ignorance is to be unaware of it. I was acutely aware that I needed to find out *what* I didn't know rather than sit and wonder as time slipped away. On that very night when I learned that psychologists would be increasingly in demand, I embarked on a plan of action to learn whether I should become one.

First things first—in the real world, what did psychologists do? I needed more than the stereotypical images. I figured that psychologists themselves would be most qualified to tell me how they filled their days. If they, too, had gotten into the field because they felt driven by a passion, how did they feel now about their chosen profession? Any regrets? Any advice?

In those days, the telephone company still sent a thick directory to every household, and I turned to mine, flipping to the yellow section of business numbers to search under "P" for psychologists. It was a rather primitive search engine, but it worked. Then I started dialing, going down the list and leaving voicemails: *"Hello, my name is Rob Douk, and I am interested in becoming a psychologist like you. I'm hoping that I can buy you lunch and we can talk about what you do, and perhaps you would agree to let me follow you around for a day to see for myself."*

I left three or four dozen such messages, and I did get a few calls back. One was from a clinical psychologist who gave me some good basic guidance. Another was a school psychologist in Long Beach named Dr. Brandon Gamble—and he told me that he would be more than pleased to show me around. We made an appointment to spend a day together at the elementary school where he was based.

At the same time, I felt that I needed to test the water in another way. It had been several years since I worked with kids in the afterschool program when I was in high school. I enjoyed it then, but I wanted to find out how I would like it now, as a college graduate, years later. If I aspired to become a psychologist specializing in children, I figured that I should find out whether I still found it energizing to be around children. Who knows? People change. I didn't want to fool myself.

So, in the spirit of due diligence, I took a part-time job at a child development center at minimum wage, which I could afford to do because I had some savings from my insurance job. This was a drop-off center for preschool and kindergarten age kids where I was involved in educational activities with them. I needed that reassurance before preparing for graduate school, which would require a lot of work in fulfilling prerequisites and studying for the admission exams. I soon felt confident that working with young people was for me.

My approach was methodical. I did not want to be impulsive about this impending change of career. You might think that I was impulsive when I bailed out of my promising insurance sales career without another job to replace it, but I made that decision, too, based on much deliberation. After all, I had spent all those lunch breaks searching for myself. I had identified why I was not happy, and I had put my future into God's hands. You might call that a leap of faith, but in Rob Douk's world even a leap is done methodically.

All along the way, I developed a plan of action. Once you know your passion and have identified a purpose, you need to continue to chart your course, turn by turn, toward your destination. You cannot make arbitrary decisions if you expect to get very far in any of life's pursuits, and that is why "plan of action" is the third "P" of business success.

LEARNING FROM THE PROS

I arrived at the elementary school early in the morning, before the school day had started, and waited outside Dr. Brandon Gamble's office. This was the same district where I had grown up, and the school was not in the best of neighborhoods. Sitting there nervously on the bench, I felt like a kid who had been sent to the principal's office, although this was another matter altogether. I was waiting for a man who had generously agreed to offer me his time and advice. As I watched the children arriving for their classes, it struck me that this gentleman got to work with kids all day long, guiding them to the services they needed so that they had a chance to be their very best.

Dr. Gamble arrived and greeted me warmly, ushering me into his office. He was a man with a big smile but an intense demeanor. And during that day, I saw plenty. I observed as he met with a parade of students, as well as teachers and administrative staff as they brainstormed on ways to better support kids at risk or in need. "And I want you to meet someone else, too," he said at one point. "Her name is Mary Ann Seng, and she's another psychologist working here in the district. In fact, she's Cambodian, too"—and, he told me, he believed that she was one of the only Cambodians working in the field on the West Coast at that time.

After spending that day with Dr. Gamble, and after finding that I enjoyed my job at the children's center, I felt confident in proceeding into graduate school at California State University, Los Angeles. I would go on to work two years directly with Ms. Seng, assisting her as a practicum student as part of my graduate work. It was during my first year working with her that I took on that job helping Omar, the Egyptian boy with autism. That's when it clicked for me. That's when I knew beyond any remaining doubt that I had chosen the right field.

As we worked together, I got to know both my new colleagues quite well. Ms. Seng had a passion for helping in the neediest of schools and was active with the police task force in combating gang violence and other troubles. I accompanied her into some of the most troubled neighborhoods. As we chatted, I learned that she, too, was a woman of faith, and I discovered that Dr. Gamble was a dedicated Christian, as well.

I had met these two good souls by picking a name from a phone book, but it turned out that we shared a passion, a purpose, and a faith. They were my introduction to the field of psychology when I was at my most impressionable, and I could not have asked for better mentors. They were the embodiment of the "P" principles that I have been describing in these chapters: Driven by a passion, they had found a meaningful vocation that turned their passion into a life purpose, and they knew how to formulate an efficient plan of action to make it all work.

If I had chosen another name in the phone book, I might have had the misfortune of working with someone who was burned out, jaded, or pessimistic, but they saw their work as a calling despite the daily challenges they faced. Their dedication led them to overcome the pressures rather than succumb to them. They felt they were making an imprint on this world by assisting these children. I observed them counseling families with compassion and patience. That was the buoyant spirit that I needed to feel. That was precisely what had been missing in my life. I knew that a power greater than me had orchestrated this.

They were the embodiment of the "P" principles that I have been describing in these chapters: Driven by a passion, they had found a meaningful vocation that turned their passion into a life purpose, and they knew how to formulate an efficient plan of action to make it all work.

I learned another enduring lesson from them, as well. They showed me the importance of making the very best decision that you can under the circumstances, with the information at hand, and not beating yourself up if you suspect later that you could have made a better call. If you used your best judgment based on the facts as you understood them, then you did indeed make the right call, despite whatever new information surfaces. That is a lesson that a lot of young psychologists—as well as a lot of entrepreneurs—should take to heart. You need to make your best choices in a timely manner. Indecision and delay can be the worst enemy, particularly in times of crisis.

WIDENING THE REACH

In my third year at the university, I secured an internship in the Los Angeles school district. By then I was specializing in ABA therapy for autism. I was studying under a bilingual program that emphasized the therapy, which was relatively new at the time. As a paid intern, I was expected to function as a full-fledged school psychologist. I felt as if I was being thrown off the deep end, but in hindsight the experience was superb.

I went on to get my master's degree and school psychology credentials, and later I would do my doctoral work in clinical psychology. After completing my master's degree, and while working on my doctorate, I began practicing professionally as a school psychologist in the Los Angeles system, soon transferring to the Garden Grove district where Ami had launched her career as a special education teacher of children with mild to moderate disabilities.

I had a heavy caseload in those districts, but in retrospect this gave me the opportunity to learn about a wide variety of interventions. In that sea of school psychologists, I was virtually the only one specializing in the ABA therapy. As a result, I handled a lot of high profile cases, and it was clear to me that my skill set was in huge demand. After seven years working in the schools, I felt a growing desire to try something different. I wanted to be able to do even more for families.

School districts have limited tools and resources. Dedicated people such as Brandon Gamble and Mary Ann Seng go above and beyond to make the most of those tools, but year after year the districts must cater to an endless stream of students in need of intervention. In some systems, each school psychologist is responsible for the welfare of a few thousand students, with caseloads in several schools. That tends to spread thin the available funding. That is not the districts' fault. Money can only go so far.

I wanted greater autonomy. Working in the schools, I felt restricted in what I could recommend to families of children with special needs, and so after much consideration I decided to move on. I wanted to go deeper in therapy and intervention, free of the bureaucracy. Nonetheless, I will always feel a great debt of gratitude to the school districts for shaping me into the professional that I am today. The schools were a great training ground, where I met a wide variety of students requiring diverse treatments.

When I went into private practice, I concentrated on the growing need in the community to treat autism through the ABA therapy. Though I was narrowing my focus, I was widening my reach. The booming demand for that service was soon evident. My referrals quickly began doubling every month. Within a year, I had thirty people on staff, and well over a hundred the next year. That has increased dramatically in the years since as BHW has expanded into multiple locations with a nationwide reach. Today, more than a thousand dedicated employees serve more than a thousand families, and the growth continues: For

When I went into private practice, I concentrated on the growing need in the community to treat autism through the ABA therapy. Though I was narrowing my focus, I was widening my reach.

several consecutive years, the company has made the Inc. 5000 list of America's fastest-growing private companies.

PEOPLE, PROCESS, PRODUCT

As part of the principle of developing a clear plan of action, three other P's play key roles in the pursuit of business success. Every entrepreneur needs to keep them top of mind. A thriving enterprise knows how to invest wisely in its *people*, its *process*, and its *product*. Those are simply good business principles. I did not invent them, but I see them through a different lens.

> *When I was a psychologist in the school districts, I strived to make the most of the abilities of the interns and the practicum students who were under my watch.*

When I was a psychologist in the school districts, I strived to make the most of the abilities of the interns and the practicum students who were under my watch. I saw this as an opportunity to serve both the collegiate students and the younger students whom we were hoping to help. The interns needed experience so they could do well in their careers. The children needed professional intervention so they could do well in life. That makes a good match.

By using those young people's talents and tapping into their enthusiasm, I knew that I could manage the caseload more effectively and efficiently. I just needed to find the appropriate process. "I'm just one person," I reasoned, "but with two interns at my side we are a team of three." The trick was to find the best mix of time and effort so that everyone would win. The interns would get a great experience, and together we would serve a greater number of kids with special needs without diluting the quality of the product—that is, the treatment that we were providing.

I kept that emphasis on people, process, and product when I moved from my role as a school psychologist into my new role as an entrepreneur. I saw those three P's as the core to running a company well, and they became the focus of our strategy at Behavioral Health Works. They continue to be the core strengths that I emphasize during executive coaching as I work with other entrepreneurs to strengthen their positions.

All around us, the world is filled with amazing people of creative talent in an array of disciplines. As individuals, they often do quite well. They land big contracts and they fill their bank accounts. They need not stand alone, however. With a little ingenuity, they could take that creativity to the next level. They could surround themselves with others who share their passions, establishing a thriving company that could replicate those talents on a larger scale, producing a greater volume of work while maintaining high standards.

It only works, though, when the right people are in the right positions and when they uniformly embrace the mission. Each employee must have the freedom to focus on what he or she does best, making the most of those natural talents. The managers must clearly define each role and find those who are the best fit, letting them do the job for which they were hired. The culture should reflect the passion upon which the company was founded. And it only works if those people follow a well-designed process that controls the quality of the product. As a business leader, you should be designing sound procedures and investing in the appropriate technology.

No business can thrive without attending to those fundamentals of people, process, and product. Let's say that you have a passion for baking and that every restaurant wants to hire you as a pastry chef. You have found your purpose. You have a job that reflects your passion. If your ambitions turn to business, however, you must think differently. If you intend to operate a pastry shop or restaurant, you will have more than a job. You will be running a business, and your own limited skills will not be enough. You need people with a variety of skills, working together systematically to produce what it takes to keep the customers coming. That is how you can grow bigger than a mom-and-pop operation. That is how you can compete on a larger scale.

ALL THE RIGHT STEPS

As I partner with other social enterprises through Douk & Co. and invest in their success, my objective is to identify people with passion who know their purpose but who have yet to figure out how to turn that purpose into a sustainable, growing business. That's where I can help, and I am qualified because that has been my journey, too. I finally identified my passion to help people and then pursued my purpose, putting in place a plan to become a school psychologist. To become an entrepreneur was also my passion, however, and so I developed a new plan to launch BHW. I had to discover the steps necessary to make the move from clinician to businessman. Those require different skill sets.

As I look to partner with other entrepreneurs, I assess their vision and mission and look for a remarkable product. I need to believe in the people and in what they are doing. If the people are a good fit and the product is a good fit, then together we can design a process that will help the business to scale. As an investor, I am looking to partner with passionate people who have an exciting innovation and who need only the right infrastructure to propel them higher.

The first step generally is to build a quality management team. It is critical to invest in the right people who are aligned on the vision and mission of the company and who understand the exact nature of the product and what it truly offers the customers. For example, the product that BHW provides is not merely therapy. In its deepest sense, the product is hope.

The senior leadership team also needs to be aligned on strategies, with the appropriate focus on what I call the three C's of customers, competitors, and core competencies. That's the way to build value. The nature of those three C's will differ for every company, but the overall strategies will be much the same.

In focusing on its customers, a successful company understands what they find valuable, whether that is good price, good service, convenience, or whatever special quality that it brings to the market. That way the company can consistently outperform the competition simply by adding more value. A successful company also thoroughly understands its competition and can pivot to address changes in market demand. Ultimately, though, it focuses on its core competencies. Nobody can be good at everything, so what does it do better than anyone else? A successful business figures out what distinguishes it from the competition and focuses on that.

Again, these are the elements of savvy business practice. Nonetheless, they are considerations that may not be readily apparent to the new entrepreneur, who has only recently entered the business world. Passion and purpose are critical but they will not take you all the way. Training and coaching can make all the difference. With a plan of action in place, success is almost inevitable.

An exercise for growth to serve a world in need:
PLAN OF ACTION

Once you have determined your passion and purpose, you will need to put together a solid plan for success. The people, the process, and the product are the three primary ingredients of a plan not only for entrepreneurial success but for dealing effectively with any significant life change. Who will be the people that you surround yourself with? What will be the process that takes you where you need to go? What is the product, or the results, that you are striving to achieve?

*In this exercise, you will work backward by identifying your **product** first: What is the goal, the service, the product that you expect will make a difference? From there, you will identify who you will need to help you reach that destination and how you will get there—that is, the **people** and the **process**. Think of those elements at a high level. The details will come later as you develop your formal business plan.*

PRODUCT

Describe what you hope to produce:

_____

_____

_____

_____

_____

_____

PEOPLE

Who will you need in your corner to achieve that product?

_____

_____

_____

_____

_____

_____

PROCESS

What are the basic steps required to get the desired results?

_____

_____

_____

_____

_____

_____

CHAPTER 9

PRIME TIME

As a man and as a businessman, I long have been taking strides toward reaching my prime. Life should be an upward trajectory of advances as we do what it takes to find success, however we define it. We must keep growing, or we risk slipping backward.

Nearly four decades ago, my family left our homeland and began the climb toward better things to come. My father saw what he had to do, and he set out on a plan of action—but the family had only just begun. It took years of hard work and dedication to get to where we are today. To grow beyond the basics of economic security, we needed to continually improve, developing new skills and identifying problems and opportunities. We succeeded only because the family held on to hope and from it gained the energy and enthusiasm to thrive. We envisioned our prime, and we did not give up.

The challenges of life are much like the challenges of business as we dream of bigger and better things. Leaders of thriving enterprises no doubt recall their startup days, when their concerns, at first, focused on mere existence and survival. They recall their hard work and dedication as they identified the problems and opportunities—and now, from the vantage point of a mature business, they recognize that they owe much of their success to maintaining the entrepreneurial spirit with which they embarked. They never gave up on their strides toward their prime.

As an entrepreneur, you have only just begun once you have discovered your passion and your purpose and determined a plan of action. You may feel a sense of direction, at long last, and you may be inspired to translate your vision into action. Even so, you probably still aren't sure what to expect. What comes next? Let's say your entrepreneurial spirit has moved you to the point of establishing a business. How do you nurture it? How do you promote its growth?

In this chapter, we will examine the steps that you should understand as an entrepreneur seeking to build a business that can fulfill your aspirations to serve others. The goal is to reach a level of prime development. In fact, the acronym PRIME summarizes the qualities of an organization that is finally positioned to contribute at its best. My advisor, Greg Arbues, shared with me that acronym and each of its crucial elements. Let's break it down to see what a business looks like in its prime.

> *The acronym PRIME summarizes the qualities of an organization that is finally positioned to contribute at its best.*

- **P**redictable profits. A company that has reached its PRIME will be generating a stream of profits that it can count on continuing as it moves forward on its mission. Those profits will be based on diverse sources so that the income stream is stable and predictable. No company can be immune to recession, but a PRIME company will be in a position to put up strong defenses against the economic forces that would threaten to bring it down.

- **R**espected and reputable. Over time, the organization becomes highly regarded for the quality of its service and products among its customers, clients, suppliers, and others in the business community. This does not happen overnight. A business must build a track record by which others will see it as reputable and reliable.

- **I**nfrastructure that is strong. A well-functioning business is like a finely tuned machine. It cannot run with missing parts, and it needs maintenance on a regular schedule to keep it humming along. When the equipment becomes outdated or worn, you replace it with something better. In my own business endeavors, I employ what I call a Total Quality Management (TQM) system, with the objective of continuous improvement. Without a strong infrastructure, you cannot attain the predictable profits and the reputation for quality that will further your growth.

- **M**anagement that is mature. A company can grow only if its management team is growing at the same time. The key players need to be constantly acquiring new skills, whether through education and training or broader experience in the field. A thriving company needs people who are bringing in new ideas. They know how to identify problems and opportunities. They know how to pivot and make the changes that will lead to personal and business growth. That is the nature of a mature management. Without it, a company grows stale and stagnant.

- **E**nergetic, energizing environment. A thriving and exciting organization will feel that way when you walk in the door. The culture will be one of high energy and innovation. It will encourage and stimulate fresh ideas, without hamstringing its people with the attitude of, "we've always done it this way, it's just fine." What if it could be better? Even if the company is meeting its numbers, could it do it faster? More cost-efficiently? The environment of a company in its prime is one of energizing innovation.

To illustrate the concept of PRIME, I displayed on the wall at BHW the image of an iceberg. Above the surface of the water, the iceberg glistens in the sunshine, but beneath the surface lies a big mass of trouble. In other words, a business that enjoys shining success likely has been through plenty of trials and tribulations that are not apparent to outside observers. While building BHW, I worked two jobs and played virtually every role, including clinician, staff trainer, and human resources person. Many of today's ambitious young people in our fast-paced age expect success to come swiftly, but they soon find out what is under of the tip of the iceberg. Success virtually always will require sacrifices. To attain PRIME takes time and effort and attention to each letter of that acronym.

Predictable profits, the first "P" of prime, were essential for BHW's growth. A smart business derives profits from a healthy mix of sources, not just one or two. BHW has a dashboard that measures what the company calls its diversification plan for accepting referrals. It benchmarks those referrals to ensure a variety of payer sources. Diversity provides assurance that the profits will hold steady even if a payer source dries up.

Reputation management also has played a key role in BHW's growth. The company monitors comments on social media, for example. It assesses the likelihood of referrals and recommendations from clients and payer sources. By maintaining quality of service, the company positions itself to scale into new regions. A good reputation builds any business. Growing responsibly means holding on to the high standards that the customers and clients expect.

I have learned that a strong infrastructure depends on a culture that emphasizes constant improvement. As a psychologist, I know that shaping behavior requires frequent feedback and reinforcement. The practice at BHW is weekly feedback on the clinical team and monthly feedback for all others. Employees assess such concerns as whether they feel valued, get clear directions, and know where they are headed. They also are asked to rate themselves on character, chemistry and competence. Their managers rate them, too. The feedback system gives employees a clear picture of where they stand. They can see whether they might expect to advance or perhaps would be better off bowing out.

Because a company cannot grow unless its management is growing at the same time, BHW has kept its people in top form with training, higher education, and certifications. The company has encouraged that environment through partnerships with universities for tuition reductions. The staff also undergoes a management development program that instructs on such matters as learning one's leadership style and the role of a manager in developing good employees into great ones. It's like a mini-MBA program. A company can always expect a return on investment from the effort to train and equip its future leaders.

BHW also has paid close attention to that last letter of PRIME, the "E" for an energetic and energizing environment. Each of the BHW locations is encouraged to develop its own regional culture and celebrations. Each of the offices, for example, has its own competitions and prizes, and anyone can nominate a fellow employee for going above and beyond in a program called "You've Got Swag!" On the BHW intranet, employees can see a distinct presence for each location that reflects the local flavor while also preserving the companywide mission and the CARES philosophy. The company recognizes that each office will be at a different stage of growth on the business lifecycle and provides the appropriate support and resources for the ascent to PRIME time.

The leaders of fast-growing companies like BHW often are asked whether their growth has come at too great a cost to their quality or their culture. Those are real concerns, and a growing business must be vigilant that it does not lose its identity as it builds to greater accomplishments. That is why understanding the elements of PRIME is essential to success: By having all the pieces in place, a business can preserve its founding culture and reputation for quality even as it grows from a mom-and-pop to a major enterprise. A company certainly needs structures but must be mindful not to become so heavy on procedure and process that it stifles the staff. BHW solicits ideas from employees about what they want to learn and promote. The human touch is irreplaceable.

Once attained, PRIME must be maintained. On average, it takes a BHW location about three years to reach PRIME. To nurture that progress, the company must anticipate each location's needs in advance. It must add staff members at the right time who are suitable

for the region's requirements and then prepare them for the ensuing growth. The company has learned through experience what works and adapts that pattern to suit each location.

I know what it is like to build a company, and I know what it is like to be a dad. To grow an organization from its infancy to maturity is a lot like parenting. I have dealt with diapers, skinned knees, and all sorts of growing pains. It is a lot of work in the early years, and it is a lot of work during the growth spurts. Even now, Ami and I are anticipating how each of our children will advance through college age and beyond. Every family needs structure and rules, just as every business needs them. Within a reliable framework, good things happen—but above all, common sense must prevail. Dedication and compassion are what nurture the growth.

I believe in the biblical principle that we should "train up a child in the way he should go, and when he is old, he will not depart from it." Our oldest child was born the year that my business was born. When Sekai arrived, my mother took me aside to tell me this: "Don't forget, Dom, that a young tree needs two strong stakes to hold it up until it can stand on its own. Make sure the ground is good, and if you want to bend it a certain way, you must do that early."

Ami and I have tried to provide that strong support. My parents each deserve an honorary MBA for their insights on what it takes to build something valuable that can grow strong to bear fruit. I'm not suggesting that business owners and managers should be paternalistic in their approach—but wisdom is wisdom.

THE EVOLUTION OF BUSINESS GROWTH

On its way to the PRIME objective, a company will experience several phases of growth, as identified in a study from the Harvard Business Review. At every step are new challenges, and meeting them successfully will advance the organization toward the next level of growth. Within any business, of course, some aspects of development will be further along the road to PRIME. The organization overall may have reached that destination, for example, while new initiatives or regional endeavors may be in their infancy with quite a way to go.

BHW Six Phases
BHW controls its growth responsibly through its tried and tested Six Phases.

Year 3	Prime: Predictable profits, recognized/respected, integrated infrastructure, mature management, enterprising energetic.	**PRIME** **400+ Cases**
24-30 Months	Decentralized management. Equip staff with detailed operational and strategic planning resources. Systems in place and rolled out to employees.	**Resources Mature** **300-399 Cases**
Year 2	Pivotal period. Managers focus on responsibly & rapidly growing within their respective environments.	**Take-Off** **200-299 Cases**
12-18 Months	Attain true economic health & plan for future generations.	**Success** **100-199 Cases**
Year 1	Start-up team transitions operations fully to regional team.	**Survival** **25-99 Cases**
0-6 Months	BHW start-up team sets up regional team for success.	**Existence** **0-25 Cases**

"Existence" is the first phase. This is the birthing stage. Here, the key challenges are to obtain customers or clients and to make good on delivering the products or services. The business is striving to establish a solid foundation and to broaden its appeal in the marketplace. At this stage, the owner is at the center of all operations and is investing heavily in time, energy, and finances. The goal is to keep the business alive without running out of start-up capital.

"Survival" is the second phase. A business that has reached this point is generating revenue and doing a reasonably good job of providing services and delivering the product. It has demonstrated the ability to hold on to customers and clients. The challenge, however, is to get beyond the breakeven point. The company needs to align the expenses with the revenue to become truly profitable. Although the staff may be growing, the owner is still the chief decision-maker at this stage.

"Success" is the phase beyond survival when the business has attained true economic health. The management has evolved and the finances have improved to the point where the company could proceed to grow further instead of simply maintaining the status quo. The leadership should be actively evaluating the business model and assessing opportunities to do more and what it would take to accomplish a bigger vision. The owner at this point could choose between expanding or to simply letting the company continue to operate as a stable and profitable source of income. He or she may wish to step aside to focus on other pursuits.

"Take-off" is the phase of ascent to still greater heights. When BHW began its boom in growth, I recall thinking: *These referrals just aren't stopping!* I soon saw that I could add staff and build profit. The company had to adjust to a bigger vision. It went from servicing a city to servicing a county to servicing all of California—and then expanding nationwide and into Canada. To provide the analytics that would be crucial to managing such rapid growth, BHW launched its Total Quality Management system during that take-off stage as well as its ClinicSoft proprietary software. The company also embarked on its vigorous management development program.

Such is the trajectory of a business in the take-off stage, a time of rapid growth and greater complexity in its structure and systems. A company must get the right people, processes, and systems in place with clear delegation of responsibilities and functions. This is a time of decentralization, when the top managers are focusing on major decisions involving strategy and vision while allowing lower level managers to attend to daily operations. The challenge is to maintain efficiency and a healthy cash flow sufficient to keep up with the pace of growth. A growing business that fails to meet these challenges will stall or could revert to prior phases in its development cycle. Many firms have failed because they took off too fast and ran out of money.

Finally, in the "resource maturity" phase, the business has attained a structure of decentralized management with well-established systems. Experienced staff members are paying close attention to the details of operational and strategic planning. The company has grown steadily and held on to the gains. It has enough talented people to take it where it wants to go. It has developed business systems that are strong and thorough. In earlier stages, the business and the owner were one and the same. Now, the business is independent of the owner in its operations and finances. Some might say the company is operating like a well-oiled machine. I prefer to think of a company in this stage as a living, breathing, healthy organism with a strong heartbeat.

Those are the typical phases of development and growth for any business, but what I have described here are simply the possibilities. There are no guarantees for growth, particularly if the business fails to meet the changing challenges along the way. Many companies that do make it out the gate become stuck at the second or third stage. They do not advance beyond the minimum required to stay in business. They continue as a "mom-and-pop"

What I have described here are simply the possibilities. There are no guarantees for growth, particularly if the business fails to meet the changing challenges along the way.

shop, plugging along until the owner dies or retires. If they do find nominal success, they could become complacent and fail to seek out further opportunities. Eventually, they could begin to backslide.

KEEPING UP THE GOOD WORK

A business that has risen through all those levels has attained PRIME—but the job still is not done. The challenge for a company that has made it to the top is to keep up the good work. It must continue innovating and growing. It must maintain the culture that led to its success. If it loses the entrepreneurial spirit upon which it was founded and that nourished its growth, it could lose sight of its values. It could die from rigidity.

With so much gained, the leadership now might fear that the company has too much to lose to continue taking the calculated risks by which the founder built the company. The company becomes set in its ways. Innovation ends. Unfortunately, the competitors still are thinking big. The real risk to a company in its prime is that those competitors will overrun it with novel ideas that customers and clients find more intriguing than the stodgy old way of doing things.

I have seen BHW grow to become a dozen times larger, or more, than its early competitors. It has done so largely by staying nimble and continually innovating to keep ahead of the curve. The company pivoted as funding sources changed, broadening and diversifying its referrals. The management grew with the times rather than complaining about the changing requirements. The company invested and prepared for each new wave. It successfully rode the surf but quickly turned to watch for the next breaker.

Organizations that have reached PRIME tend to be large and complex with systems in place, but big ships can take more time to maneuver, and they, too, can sink. Business systems must be inspected regularly to ensure that they are adequate and functioning well. The officers must remain vigilant, maintaining clear communication all the way from the front office to the shop floor—from the helm to the rudder. They must be constantly scanning the horizon so that they can turn in time, and they must maintain the appropriate speed and pace for the current conditions. They need to be able to see what's coming, or, like the Titanic, it can be too late.

As I consult with other entrepreneurs, we talk about strategies for staying ahead. To remain relevant, a company must be clear about its values and stay true to them. As the company grows and adjusts to the times, the leadership must make decisions that are aligned with those values. The values need to be communicated throughout the organization so that they are central to the culture of the workplace. The leaders must do more than recite some mission statement by rote. They must show by their actions and their attitudes that they abide by those values. Nobody should doubt where the company stands. Everyone should understand the brand.

As I consult with other entrepreneurs, we talk about strategies for staying ahead. To remain relevant, a company must be clear about its values and stay true to them. As the company grows and adjusts to the times, the leadership must make decisions that are aligned with those values.

Not only must they understand it, they also need to embrace it. They should feel it. This is the concept of "internal brand alignment," which I prefer to think of as connecting the heads with the hearts.

Intellectual buy-in is essential, of course. The staff must have a working knowledge of the values, mission, and vision of the brand and be able to express clearly what the company is doing. Emotional buy-in, however, is what will inspire everyone involved, from the top managers to the lowest level employees, to do their utmost for the company. They know what the company is doing and they know why it is doing it and they want to help do it. When everyone is aligned on the brand and the vision and sees it as their mission, the company not only can stay ahead but is likely to forge ahead.

Starbucks is one example of a company that has aligned its brand into its culture. Starbucks is all about ambience, and the top management knows that's a big part of what the customer is buying. The managers also pass along that message to employees all the way down the line. The emphasis is on servant leadership, warm relationships, collaboration, and openness.[3] Whether you are in New York or Modesto or New Mexico, you expect a similar quirky atmosphere and service with a smile from your barista. The employees understand what the culture is meant to be, and those who embrace it will perform it. Starbucks has long served up the brand that it knows will work, and that brand is more than the coffee.

That's what I mean by a culture that is in the heart as well as the head. "Culture" is not just some fluffy, feel-good thing. It is good business. When you groom a culture that advances sales and profits, and when everyone from top to bottom in the organization wants to be part of the action, you will be in far better shape to take on the competition.

---

3   Edward Ferguson, "Starbucks Coffee Company's Organizational Culture," Panmore Institute, January 31, 2017, http://panmore.com/starbucks-coffee-company-organizational-culture.

Internal Brand Alignment

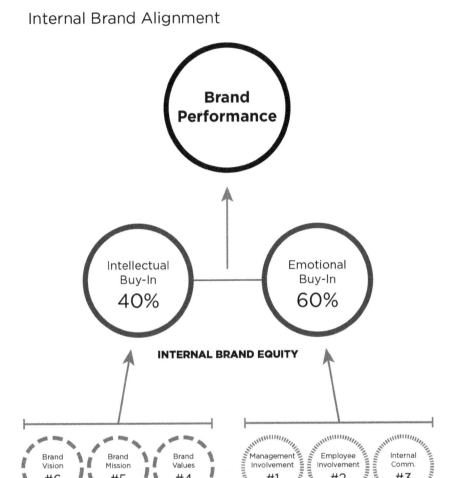

Information adapted from Professor Prem Shamdasani, PhD - Academic Director of The NUS Executive MBA Program and Co-Director of the Stanford-NUS Executive Program in International Management

TOTAL QUALITY MANAGEMENT

At Douk & Co., I coach other business leaders and entrepreneurs on how they can build toward PRIME. We talk about adopting total quality management like the proprietary TQM system that I established at Behavioral Health Works. It functions like the dashboard of a car or an airplane, which has dials and indicators of various sorts that reveal what is going on. If you are going too fast, you can adjust to the conditions. If you are running out of gas, you will see that well before you are left stranded. The management system helps you make the right decisions as you navigate through uncertainties and challenges.

Total Quality Management

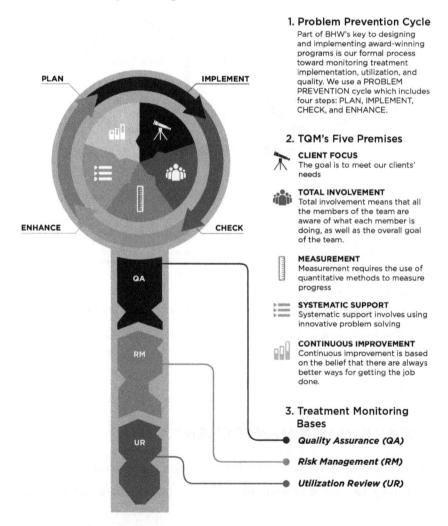

1. Problem Prevention Cycle

Part of BHW's key to designing and implementing award-winning programs is our formal process toward monitoring treatment implementation, utilization, and quality. We use a PROBLEM PREVENTION cycle which includes four steps: PLAN, IMPLEMENT, CHECK, and ENHANCE.

2. TQM's Five Premises

CLIENT FOCUS
The goal is to meet our clients' needs

TOTAL INVOLVEMENT
Total involvement means that all the members of the team are aware of what each member is doing, as well as the overall goal of the team.

MEASUREMENT
Measurement requires the use of quantitative methods to measure progress

SYSTEMATIC SUPPORT
Systematic support involves using innovative problem solving

CONTINUOUS IMPROVEMENT
Continuous improvement is based on the belief that there are always better ways for getting the job done.

3. Treatment Monitoring Bases

Quality Assurance (QA)

Risk Management (RM)

Utilization Review (UR)

Total quality management, in general, is the philosophy of continuous improvement that many industries have adopted as they have sought to remain competitive. It should involve every department, whether it is operations, sales, the production line, or customer service. To excel, you need regular and reliable feedback. You must be able to measure performance and progress, for better or for worse. You need metrics and scorecards so that you know when it is time to pivot.

In effect, as an entrepreneur you have built a machine, and it will need new gears now and then that will mesh well with every other part. You must oil it regularly, or it will wear out long before it has served your purpose. As time passes, you likely will need to bring in new and better machines as technology and expectations change. If something is broken, you will need time to fix it before the problem worsens. With total quality management, you can find out with a glance at the dash whether anything is malfunctioning. In fact, you can log in to your dashboard and run your company from miles away, if necessary. You gain flexibility and freedom.

Total quality management, in general, is the philosophy of continuous improvement that many industries have adopted as they have sought to remain competitive. It should involve every department, whether it is operations, sales, the production line, or customer service.

Early in your entrepreneurial life, you likely will be doing most everything, day to day. You will be the HR expert, the finance expert, the production line guru, and more. In time, you will hire others to fill those roles, but life happens: People move away, or they get ill, or resign, or for whatever reason are no longer available. For each function, you need a process that you can depend on so that anyone you plug into a particular spot could do the job reasonably well. It is much easier to control the process than the people. If you have a phenomenal process, you will get great results even if you cannot always keep an A+ employee on the job all the time.

As your company grows, you will have increasingly more people and processes to manage, and you can keep things simpler by examining those metrics, even if you cannot be in the office. They will be your guide to the health of the organization so that you do not need to be micromanaging. You only step in when your dashboard indicates trouble. You can devote most of your time to watching out for the big stuff, carrying forth your vision and moving forward with confidence.

READY FOR PRIME TIME

Once your business has reached PRIME, you will want to sustain that status as you continually improve operations through your total quality management. Whether your plan is to eventually sell the business or to continue it to the next generation as a family legacy, you will need to focus on the fundamentals of how to build value.

Successful companies generally will want to put in place the necessary management and training so that they can scale further. Growth should center on the services or products that differentiate the company as special in the marketplace, as opposed to those that are perceived as common commodities. The company also should identify which of its services are easiest to teach and to replicate at other locations. In other words, the best way to scale is to do more of what comes easily to you and what you do especially well.

At BHW, for example, the logical focus for scaling has been its applied behavioral analysis services. The ABA services are teachable. The company can easily recruit therapists and put them through its board-approved training, and they are providing a specialized service for which the company made a name for itself. It also offers such services as counseling and speech and occupational therapy, but those are commonly available from other providers. BHW recognized early the unmet need for ABA therapy and focused intently on developing its training system. The company thereby grew rapidly on the strength of a service that differentiated it and that it could replicate readily.

As you evaluate your company's potential for growth, look first for low-risk opportunities. Consider the products and services that you already provide and establish how you might make further inroads into the marketplace. You certainly can diversify and develop plans to explore other lines of business that are medium to higher risk, but first make the most of what you already know and do well. Go for your low-hanging fruit that is hanging lush and ripe, within easy reach. You grew it well, so do it again. If you spread those seeds far and wide in good soil, you soon will find the fruit hanging heavily on other branches, too, and many others will be eager to partake of your harvest.

Such was the case with ABA services. As the leader of our expanding company, I had to make sure that we did not lose our momentum. Companies should resist the temptation to spread themselves thin as they get referrals for a variety of new services in other locations. Undertaking different endeavors so soon in new regions takes up resources and diverts energy from the primary specialty. That is not the path to robust growth. Establishing new management and leadership takes time. It takes even longer when developing new products and services. That is why growth should focus on proven, reliable business models. Our best bet was to go ever deeper into ABA.

Meanwhile, I also developed what I called my innovation lab to cook up new ideas. I nonetheless wanted to brainstorm on services and products that we did not yet offer and on their potential for growth in new geographic regions. Knowing what you do well does not mean you should ignore ideas and opportunities. A growing company should invest in research and development and beta testing.

We were able to explore growth strategies both vertically and horizontally, as well as geographically and culturally. How would we respond as we encountered companies offering compatible services and those offering similar services? How might we consider expanding globally into regions with systems and values different than what we knew in the United States? We studied, for example, how our business model might work in Singapore, and we concluded at the time that we would need to wait a few years because of funding regulations and because ABA services were only starting to gain the attention of pediatrician groups there. In the United States, the services started in the schools, was funded by the regional centers, and then became a medical model under commercial insurance. ABA was developing similarly in Singapore but had not reached that final stage needed for ample resources and funding.

I kept in mind another fundamental for building value: A strong business generates recurring revenue. In doing so, it exhibits the predictable process that is one of the hallmarks of a company in PRIME. Recurring revenue can come in the form of a subscriptions model or a simplifier model. A subscriptions model works like a magazine: The consumer pays to get something on a regular basis. Under a simplifier model, the consumer pays up front for a product or service needed regularly so that he or she does not need to bother scheduling it again and again. The model makes life simpler for the consumer, in other words, and brings in a steady and more predictable stream of revenue for the company.

With either the subscription or simplifier model, you can bank on that money coming in, and you know in advance the demand for your product or service. That gives you a better picture of your likely overhead costs, and you can budget accordingly.

Autism often requires years of treatment. We can dream of the day when there will be a cure, but we are not there yet. BHW knew that the demand for its services would be continuous. Although it had a good record of discharging patients faster than other providers, the company still could predict how long a patient was likely to remain in the program. It therefore could depend upon a recurring revenue model for business growth. In some regions, the company has found that clients appreciate a contract model to streamline services. With a contract, the client gets convenience and efficiency from a company with a proven track record, and the business gets the predictable revenue that it needs to scale.

Frankly, most businesses that aspire to help people in need can expect to find a recurring demand for their services. The world's troubles seem to be compounding, not diminishing, and some of those situations are so dire that a provider might prefer to go out of business rather than see so much suffering. Those needs are not likely to disappear anytime soon. We face an increasing demand for the ingenuity and compassion of entrepreneurs ready to rise to the occasion. Those who operate healthy and thriving businesses will be in a better position to help.

On the way to greater growth, a company must keep in mind the need to diversify sufficiently so that it does not become overly dependent on just a few customers, suppliers, or employees. To build a company that relies too much on any entity means facing a big risk that if that entity disappears, the business will vanish, too. This is the principle of nonreliance, and you must consider it carefully as you prepare to scale.

What happens, for example, if a major supplier of services or materials for your enterprise suddenly shuts its doors? Do you have an alternative ready to go? What if your best employee decides to move to Kalamazoo and your business is based in Burbank? Let's say a serious injury puts your top sales person out of commission: Who stands ready to step into the gap? That is why you should rely more on the process rather than on the person so that any qualified employee whom you plug into a given position would likely do well. Similarly, if 80 percent of your business relies on Google or Twitter, you have issues. If you drop that basket, you break most of your eggs.

The objective should be growth with control. As BHW pursued initiatives across the nation, the company was strategic about being one of the top players in every region that it serviced. It would strive to represent a significant percentage of a health plan's patients, for example. That status gave the company a seat at the table to help determine how to improve services and technologies and decide which metrics to use in measuring quality of care. As a significant player with a reputation as a pioneer in its field, the company gained more influence and control over treatment standards for families. By building its market share, BHW was positioning itself to further revolutionize the field. A company that is proving itself will get the opportunity to prove a lot more. As it grows, its voice gets louder.

Even as the organization itself strives to gain control, however, the founder should not become the controlling sort. Entrepreneurs often are overprotective of their baby to the point of wanting to know every detail about what is going on. Often that is why they hit a wall and cannot get to PRIME. They fail to put in place a mature management that they trust.

The goal should be to foster an organization that continuously improves without relying solely on the founder. He or she needs the creative freedom to look for innovations several years ahead and will be more valuable to the company that way. The managers should focus on the day-to-day operations. As a good steward, of course, the founder should be checking in regularly on how the company is faring, but that oversight can be accomplished from afar. As the company hums along like a well-maintained machine, it spits out data that the founder can monitor online. If anything is going wrong, the metrics soon reveal the problem.

I founded BHW with the objective that it would be a transparent and nimble operation that could pivot easily to face challenges and pursue opportunities. To accomplish that, I needed to be on top of things to get the best possible view, not so buried in things that I couldn't see. In fact, I wanted to attain such clarity that I could monitor the company from thousands of miles away if necessary. That became possible through our TQM system, by which I could examine the dashboard. I could tell at a glance if it was all systems go.

Eventually I no longer needed to personally interact with the customers and clients. My top managers stood strong for me, diligently addressing the details. My chief executive team of Brandon Douk and Michael Zhe, along with my director and management level staff, allowed me to be the visionary that I was created to be. I knew that they would take good care of the families who entrusted their care to us, day by day, while I looked for opportunities to reach out to even more families. I could focus on what I did best. As an entrepreneur, that should remain your primary role. That is how your business grows, and that is how you grow, too.

As a student pilot, I learned the importance of the preflight inspections and checks. My instructors taught me how to read the dashboard gauges that would indicate whether something was amiss. I conducted the various points of routine inspection around the plane. It is my responsibility as pilot to ensure that all is in good working order—and that includes me. I have learned that pilot error causes many more problems than equipment malfunction, and so I must stay well-rested, alert, and always on course.

I am not a mechanic. I do not know how to design or repair engines. I don't personally perform the maintenance, although I make sure that it gets done on schedule. Others can do those things far better than me, and I don't hover over their shoulders. What I can do is fly. I can make that well-maintained machine take to the sky.

Entrepreneurs, like pilots, must get ready for flight. They need the facts to exercise good judgment. I have been trained as a psychologist in a field that puts a priority on the scientific evidence behind recommendations for care. As a business leader, however, I also know that good care requires teamwork. I can depend on others to deliver to me what I need to know. My job is to make sure that the facts support the big picture and contribute to the organization's founding vision and its trajectory of growth. My job is to chart the course and fly.

I carry that mindset with me as I work with fellow entrepreneurs to develop their business prospects. As socialpreneurs, we must maintain our vision and growth if we aspire to provide the very best of care for the needs of the world. By growing stronger together, we truly will be ready for PRIME time.

An exercise for growth:
PRIME TIME

A successful entrepreneur should be striving to advance the organization until it reaches PRIME status and then maintain it there. The acronym stands for the following key attributes:

Predictable profits

Respected and reputable

Infrastructure that is strong

Management that is mature

Energetic, energizing environment

In this exercise, you will chart where you are in respect to each attribute. Review the definitions of those attributes as presented in this chapter, and then determine the improvements that you need so that you can get to PRIME status. Rate each attribute on a scale of 1 to 10.

PREDICTABLE PROFITS

1	2	3	4	5	6	7	8	9	10

Rating

Action Plan

3 months

_____

_____

12 months

_____

_____

3 Years

_____

_____

RESPECTED AND REPUTABLE

1	2	3	4	5	6	7	8	9	10

Rating

Action Plan

3 months

_____

_____

12 months

_____

_____

3 Years

_____

_____

INFRASTRUCTURE THAT IS STRONG

| 1 | 2 | 3 | 4 | 5 | 6 | 7 | 8 | 9 | 10 |

Rating

Action Plan

3 months

_____

_____

12 months

_____

_____

3 Years

_____

_____

MANAGEMENT THAT IS MATURE

| 1 | 2 | 3 | 4 | 5 | 6 | 7 | 8 | 9 | 10 |

Rating

Action Plan

3 months

_____

_____

12 months

_____

_____

3 Years

_____

_____

ENERGETIC, ENERGIZING ENVIRONMENT

| 1 | 2 | 3 | 4 | 5 | 6 | 7 | 8 | 9 | 10 |

Rating

Action Plan

3 months

_____

_____

12 months

_____

_____

3 Years

_____

_____

Additional Resources:

To learn more and for guidance on how to complete the following additional resources, please visit **drdouk.com**.

WHAT IS STRATEGY

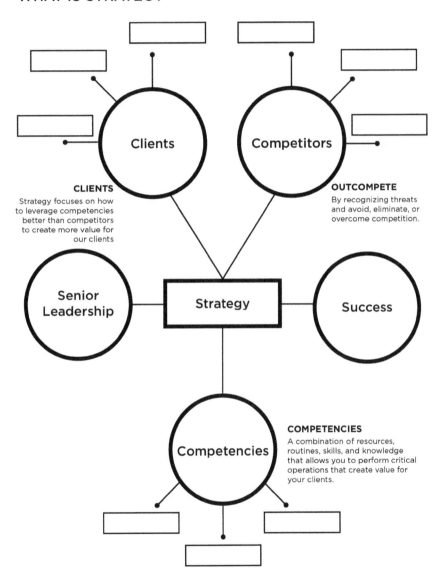

CLIENTS
Strategy focuses on how to leverage competencies better than competitors to create more value for our clients

OUTCOMPETE
By recognizing threats and avoid, eliminate, or overcome competition.

COMPETENCIES
A combination of resources, routines, skills, and knowledge that allows you to perform critical operations that create value for your clients.

Information adapted from Kulwant Singh, PhD - Professor of Strategy and Policy, and Deputy Dean at the NUS Business School.

HOW TO CREATE VALUE

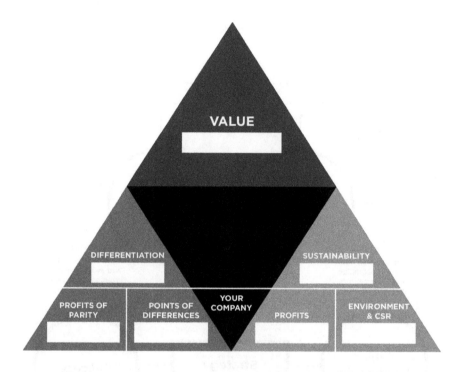

Information adapted from Professor Prem Shamdasani, PhD - Academic Director of The NUS Executive MBA Program and Co-Director of the Stanford-NUS Executive Program in International Management

INTERNAL BRAND ALIGNMENT

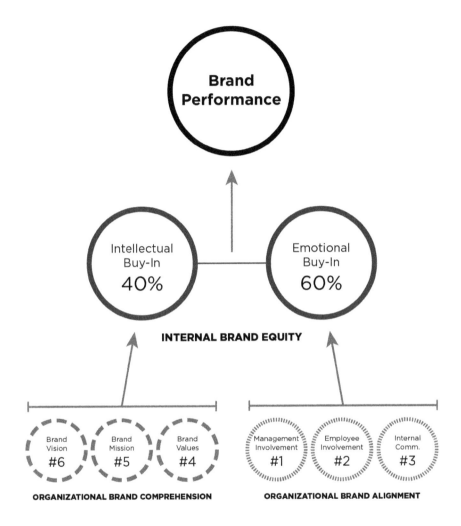

TOTAL QUALITY MANAGEMENT

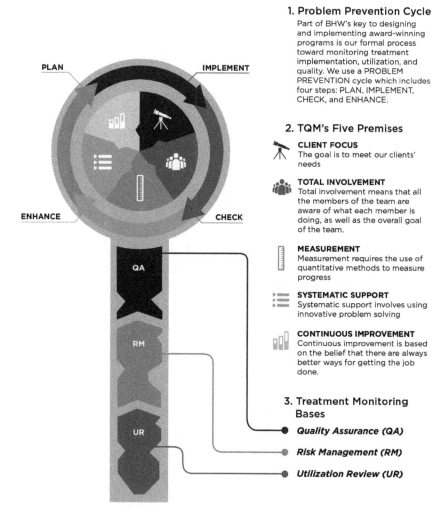

PLAN

IMPLEMENT

ENHANCE

CHECK

QA

RM

UR

1. Problem Prevention Cycle

Part of BHW's key to designing and implementing award-winning programs is our formal process toward monitoring treatment implementation, utilization, and quality. We use a PROBLEM PREVENTION cycle which includes four steps: PLAN, IMPLEMENT, CHECK, and ENHANCE.

2. TQM's Five Premises

CLIENT FOCUS
The goal is to meet our clients' needs

TOTAL INVOLVEMENT
Total involvement means that all the members of the team are aware of what each member is doing, as well as the overall goal of the team.

MEASUREMENT
Measurement requires the use of quantitative methods to measure progress

SYSTEMATIC SUPPORT
Systematic support involves using innovative problem solving

CONTINUOUS IMPROVEMENT
Continuous improvement is based on the belief that there are always better ways for getting the job done.

3. Treatment Monitoring Bases

Quality Assurance (QA)

Risk Management (RM)

Utilization Review (UR)

CHAPTER 10

PAYING IT FORWARD

A scene from the California shore, circa 2002: Three young surfer guys sit on the tailgate of a pickup truck in the parking lot of a Trader Joe's in the early evening, partaking of ice cream sandwiches. They have spent the day riding the waves at the Wedge in Newport Beach, and now they begin talking about life after college. They are imagining what might be, and their dreams are the big ones of youth.

That was me, with my friends James and Ed, whom I had met through a campus youth group. As we sat there enjoying the ocean breeze, our flip-flops dangling from our feet, it struck me that we soon would be graduating—and what would be the next big wave coming in?

"So what comes next?" I asked, broadly. James said he figured we had better get back to campus. He needed to finish a paper but suggested we might cruise around town a while first.

Ed understood the drift of my words and my mood. "Yeah, we have a lot to figure out, for sure," he said. "You've got to wonder what God has in store for us."

"Oh," said James. He licked the edge of his sandwich. "But I know this!" he added brightly. "If he gives us more days like this, I'll be one happy dude!"

"I want to do big things," I said, "and that means I've got to make it big. You can't do anything without money."

"Really?" said James. "I mean, it seems money just gets in the way a lot of the time and that's all people think about."

I smiled at him and pointed to his ice cream. "Well, it took money to buy that," I said, "and, hey, I'm thinking this is a pretty nice truck you have here!" I stood up in the bed of the pickup and looked at the row of lights down the boulevard. "I think about all the great things we could do, but you need money for that, too."

"So why not both?" Ed said. "We could go out and make some money and then use it to help people."

"Yeah. It would be like paying it back," James said, getting into the spirit. "There are a lot of folks hurting out there."

"Or paying it forward," I said. "It's not like you owe money to somebody, like when you bought this truck. It's more like you're grateful and want to do for somebody else what somebody did for you."

"Well, I guess we all know what God had done for us," Ed said. "We owe it to him, anyway."

I jumped to the pavement. "Maybe we could build empires here on earth," I said, "so that we can make a real difference someplace, like where people are struggling."

"Sort of like a life mission," said James.

"Like doing something big for God to use," said Ed.

"Yeah, like that. We've got to make that happen," I said, opening the passenger door. It was time for us to get going. But I knew that I wasn't just along for the ride.

Back then, I hadn't even found my own passion and purpose in life, let alone discovered how whatever I might build could help the world. I just knew that I wanted to make money and do big things. Come graduation day, I would start out by seeking my fortune at an insurance company, where I would be profoundly unhappy. I had a long way to go. But I was on my way.

> *It was time for us to get going. But I knew that I wasn't just along for the ride.*

In the decade to come, as I pursued higher degrees, worked as a school psychologist, and started my own business, I would think often about that conversation in the parking lot. I felt that I needed to be true to those words we had shared that day. Much was being given to me and my family. It was time that I lived up to my vow to reach out to the world. It was time to become a socialpreneur and to pay it forward.

GIVING IS GOOD BUSINESS

"Paying it forward" is the final essential principle for business success. My friend James was right: We must think about more than just the money. We give money true value by the manner in which we use it, and it is our mutual responsibility to devote a portion of what comes our way to the betterment of our world.

If someone helps you out on the condition that you must pay it back, you are merely engaging in a transaction. You have been extended a loan. If someone helps you out without requiring repayment, however, you still have an obligation. To whom much is given, much is required. We must pay forward the blessings in some manner to someone else.

We give money true value by the manner in which we use it, and it is our mutual responsibility to devote a portion of what comes our way to the betterment of our world.

If you have been successful at business, you may want to believe that good fortune is a reflection of all your hard work. Yes, you did put a lot of effort into your work, and you do deserve credit. And you also should put a lot of effort into your giving. Many people are struggling through no fault of their own. If each of us felt an obligation to find a way to pay forward the good things that come to us, a mighty wave of well-being soon would sweep the world.

Paying it forward is simply good business. While a company is adding value for the community, it also can be adding profits. The mentality of paying it forward signals to one and all that the business puts a premium on innovative and forward thinking. Such an enterprise will attract those who value that perspective. They want to work for the company because they want to be part of something that matters. They believe in the product or the service. They feel that they are part of a movement. That passion translates into dedication, which translates into growth, which translates into profit.

Most any business can find a way to play that role. A pen manufacturer, for example, could donate some of those pens for the cause of literacy and let every employee know that this gesture of paying it forward will be part of the company's mission. The staff will feel pleased to be part of that initiative. As the culture improves, productivity improves. In effect, paying it forward becomes an investment in forward thinking. A prevailing attitude of "let's add value for everyone we touch" will become quite an advantage over the competition. It helps the community, and it helps the bottom line.

> *In effect, paying it forward becomes an investment in forward thinking. A prevailing attitude of "let's add value for everyone we touch" will become quite an advantage over the competition.*

Larger organizations often engage in corporate social responsibility programs. Nestlé is an example of a company that does this well. Rather than charging into a community with bulldozers to build a plant, the company takes the time to partner with local entrepreneurs and farmers and others. It hires local tradespeople. The company makes sure that the community is on board with the project so that everyone has a stake in its success. Corporate responsibility calls for such a collaborative approach. Before setting up shop, a company should win a community's approval, and that starts with respect and the demonstrated desire to leave that community better.[4]

---

4   "Nestlé in society: Creating Shared Value and meeting our commitments 2016," Nestlé, March 2017, http://www.nestle.com/asset-library/documents/library/documents/corporate_social_responsibility/nestle-in-society-summary-report-2016-en.pdf.

If an entrepreneur starts out by identifying a community problem that he or she wants to solve and manages to do the job well, the profits will come. Exemplary service is the way to outcompete everybody. An entrepreneur with a great idea whose head and heart are in the right place can be confident that the business will be in demand. If, at the same time, the entrepreneur develops some good business savvy, it will be hard not to make money.

SPREADING THE HOPE

It was in the spirit of social responsibility that Ami and I founded our nonprofit Hope Out Loud, once it was clear that Behavioral Health Works was succeeding. The company was only a year old but already was growing rapidly, and we wanted to ensure that we didn't lose sight of the founding passion for helping others. We wanted the business to accomplish much more than supporting our family. Hope Out Loud felt like the path that we were meant to take.

At that point, in 2011, I was only just beginning to operate BHW full-time. Ami and I both still were working for the Garden Grove school district. I didn't want to leave a full-time job until I knew BHW would be a success. The signs were good, though, that we had been given something special. If the company kept its trajectory, it clearly could become quite large and lucrative. We looked at our lives. We didn't want to become the kind of family that basked in material success. We dreamed of building an organization bigger than BHW that would touch others and spread hope on a larger scale.

As health professionals, we wanted an organization that could extend behavioral services, such as those provided by BHW, around the world and train clinicians and teachers in countries in need of such services. We wanted to teach sanitation and other health essentials, as well. Because a lack of clean water is a particularly urgent issue worldwide, we wanted to start by providing wells in strategic locations throughout Southeast Asia. That is why two of our initiatives were in the categories of *health services* and *clean water*.

We designated our third category, *hope*, to address a variety of other needs. As just one example, we would fight human trafficking by teaching skills such as knitting and other crafts so that the potential victims, mostly girls and young women, might sustain a living and avoid falling into the clutches of those who would exploit them. Such skills also help to prevent survivors from falling back into the cycle of enslavement.

Ultimately, the goal of Hope Out Loud is to help families meet basic needs and to provide them with opportunities to pull themselves up and reach for something better, as my own family was able to do long ago during our refugee years. Hope Out Loud is our way of paying it forward.

Getting personally involved in such outreach efforts will pay dividends to the soul. One might argue that cutting a check to a relief organization is the most efficient way to help, and certainly that money will go a long way. It isn't cheap to book seats on an airplane to send a group overseas for a week.

> *The goal of Hope Out Loud is to help families meet basic needs and to provide them with opportunities to pull themselves up and reach for something better, as my own family was able to do long ago during our refugee years.*

Those who operate mission trips, however, will be quick to tell you that the givers can get as much out of the experience as the receivers. You cannot put a price on the heart to heart connection. The giver gets a life-changing perspective on the needs of humanity that he or she could never have gained by staying home. The receiver observes that someone from far away truly cares enough to lend a hand literally. I believe that serving people is a mandate for all of us and that what we do for others will come back to us in multiples. We of course must give joyously and selflessly without expectation of anything in return, but the principle of paying it forward will ultimately benefit each of us personally because it benefits mankind. It is truly an investment and a smart strategy, whether for your business or for your soul.

The members of my family have become personally involved in the endeavors of Hope Out Loud, with the intent of growing that outreach. We work as a team and do our best, although the logistics that we encounter can be frustrating at times when we come face to face with the sheer extent of human need. We are still in our early years with the organization and continuing to develop the best strategies. Every step counts.

My parents have taken much of the initiative, with Ami orchestrating the many details of contacts, travel, and arrangements. She has been the backbone of the effort. I have been on trips to train pediatricians and educators on ABA treatment for autism at hospitals and schools in Mexico, Cambodia, and India, with the goal of helping them to launch sustainable programs. My father has headed up our water well projects and my mother our "hope" initiatives in Cambodia and elsewhere in Southeast Asia. We have been looking into an outreach in Rwanda, as well.

I became aware of the human trafficking problem years ago during that mission trip that I led to Thailand, not long after graduating from college. When we started Hope Out Loud, we determined that we would make it one of our priorities to fight that blight on humanity. My mother, who is skillful at knitting and crocheting, took the initiative to lead workshops to help young women learn a marketable craft and a livelihood. It gives them an alternative. It gives them hope.

Meanwhile, my father's lifelong skills as a handyman and problem solver have proved valuable as he has revisited his homeland to give back. He has singlehandedly assembled a team of half a dozen workers who regularly dig wells where they are most needed, often near schools. At first, he did a lot of the manual work himself to understand every aspect of the process. His team has been equipped with the tools, materials and knowledge to continue serving the citizens of Cambodia, a land where my father once rescued his family from tyranny. It would be understandable, because of that troubled past, for him to feel uncomfortable even today, as if a suspicious government might somehow see treachery in what he does. He does it anyway. Fear will not stop him.

Back home, my brother and sister have been actively involved in organizing and preparing for our annual gala in January whereby we spread the word about these Hope Out Loud initiatives and celebrate them. This is truly a family effort—and by *family*, I mean the corporate family, too, and the many donors who have supported our cause. Every BHW employee has been welcome at the gala to feel connected with the global work of the foundation. They learn about the programs that we are involved in. They hear about how many wells we have dug. It is gratifying to know that the work you do locally has a ripple effect globally. Typically, we rent a yacht for the gala and enjoy a black-tie evening of food and dancing. It is truly a celebration of possibilities. And more often than not, as the evening ends, my brother, sister and I join the volunteers to pack up the boxes, still dressed in our finest, and stop for a breakfast burrito on the way home. I wouldn't have it any other way.

> *Paying it forward is the fulfillment of the five P's. It is the principle that makes it all worthwhile.*

Paying it forward is the fulfillment of the five P's. It is the principle that makes it all worthwhile. I didn't get into the field of psychology to make money. I had already discovered during my abbreviated insurance sales career that there must be more to life than that. I entered the field because I had found my passion and my purpose—and it turned out that helping others in that way was an opportunity to develop an amazing and lucrative business. In a world of many needs, there are countless ways to help. It pays to care about one another.

An exercise for growth:
PAYING IT FORWARD

When someone does you a good turn and you pay it back, you can't really call it a gift. It was simply a transaction. But when someone does you a good turn and you pay it forward to help others in need, you could be starting a chain reaction of beneficence.

In this exercise, you can identify how you can best be involved in the art of giving:

What are the needs within the communities where you spend most of your time? (Your list may include food and shelter for the homeless, after-school programs for youth at risk, etc.)

_____

_____

_____

_____

_____

_____

What resources does your company have that will meet one or all of the needs from the previous question? (Examples can include financial donations, staff volunteer, specialized skills, etc.)

_____

_____

_____

_____

_____

_____

Now, identify which community needs could best be addressed by your company.

_____

_____

_____

_____

_____

_____

Who from your company will be the key players on a committee to address those needs?

_____

_____

_____

_____

_____

_____

How will you meet those needs, and how often during the workweek will you be engaged in this endeavor?

_____

_____

_____

_____

_____

_____

At each step, from launching the campaign to completing it, who will be responsible for approvals and providing support?

_____

_____

_____

_____

_____

_____

LET'S GET TO WORK

The temple of Angkor Wat in northwest Cambodia has stood since the 12th century as testimony to the grandeur of the Khmer Empire, once a dominant culture in Southeast Asia. Today the temple has become a national symbol, depicted on the country's flag. Tourists shiver in awe at the beauty and harmony of the temple's architecture and the elaborate bas-reliefs that adorn it. This is the Cambodia that was.

The tourists also come to shiver at another monument to the past, this one a Buddhist stupa that is several miles from the capital of Phnom Penh. The ornate tower rises two hundred feet over a cratered field that once was an orchard. The tower is filled with human skulls, many of them crushed, that stare out from glass panels. They were exhumed from mass graves nearby, where bones still wash up from the ground in the heavy rains. The country has many such graves. This, too, is the Cambodia that was.

Life goes on, but we must not forget the past—neither our seasons of horror nor our seasons of glory. The Killing Fields Museum of Cambodia sees its mission as helping to support humanitarian, cultural, and educational projects. It does more than catalogue a crime against humanity. It honors the fortitude of humanity.

The most enduring memorial of all is to build diligently and fearlessly toward a better world. Such is the goal of social entrepreneurship. Good people, working together, can overcome the challenges to make a profound difference. Small steps can climb high. The modest contributions of sincere hearts can ripple through generations and become a movement.

> *The most enduring memorial of all is to build diligently and fearlessly toward a better world. Such is the goal of social entrepreneurship.*

I am honored to count myself in that corps of fearless socialpreneurs. As the founder of Douk & Co., I seek now to partner with others who, in one way or another, are bettering the world. I am eager to meet others of like mind and to come alongside them on their journeys. Together, we can build toward greater success. Together, we can do more.

In these pages, I have shared ten fundamentals of good living and good business. Five of them are foundations for a balanced life. Five are principles that every business leader and entrepreneur should take to heart. As socialpreneurs, we need all of them so that we can live a meaningful life, without regrets. We need to make it our business to leave the world better than we found it.

There is much to do. Let's get to work.

OUR SERVICES

Douk & Company pairs entrepreneurs and CEOs with the resources and expertise they need to build companies of extraordinary value.

WHO WE ARE

Douk & Co. is a growth investment firm that partners and networks with like-minded leaders to build profitable businesses that also profit society. Our advisors, who have a range of sector expertise and experience, promote smart and efficient strategic changes with minimal bureaucracy. A technology-focused investor, Douk & Co. offers a suite of resources that incorporate best practices into a natural workflow environment. We equip leaders at all levels to develop their strategic focus with the flexibility to pivot as the business climate and organizational needs change.

OUR APPROACH

We partner with entrepreneurs and CEOs to scale their existing business to new heights. Douk & Co. is not a venture capitalist group, private equity firm, or traditional management consultant. We are not a firm that manages capital, nor do we acquire companies using raised capital. You pay no consultation fees as we are not a fee-for-service firm, nor do we consider ourselves consultants. When you decide to join Douk & Co., we become your partner. Douk & Co. funds all its own investments, and our dedicated team rolls up its sleeves to work closely with you.

THE PROCESS

Depending on your business needs, we will provide the following services as part of our executive partnership suite of tailored solutions:

- Strategy and Forecasting
- Business Improvement Plan and Implementation
- Operational Fine Tuning and Maximizing Efficiency
- Human Resources Audit and Guidance
- Financial Planning and Forecasting
- Audit and Risk Management
- Board of Advisors Establishment
- Marketing, Branding, and Social Media Integration
- Executive Coaching and Education

INDUSTRY FOCUS

Our agile executive team partners in hand-selected industries where we find growth. Additionally, we typically partner with companies that achieve not only financial returns but also significant measurable social benefits.

- Technology

- Manufacturing

- Real Estate

- Winery

- Industrial

- Healthcare

- Finance

- Non-Profit

- Executive Coaching and Education

BE CONSIDERED FOR PARTNERSHIP

Douk & Co.'s goal is to identify companies to add to its portfolio who represents the top thought leaders and innovators throughout the business world today. Please go to douk.co and fill out our "Be Considered for Partnership" form. A member from our Global Partnership team will be in touch with you if you qualify.

LET'S CONNECT

Web douk.co; drdouk.com

Email rob@drdouk.com

SOCIAL MEDIA

Facebook facebook.com/dr.douk/

Twitter twitter.com/drdouk

Instagram instagram.com/dr.douk/

LinkedIn linkedin.com/in/drdouk/

A Special Offer from ForbesBooks

Other publications bring you business news. Subscribing to *Forbes* magazine brings you business knowledge and inspiration you can use to make your mark.

- Insights into important business, financial and social trends
- Profiles of companies and people transforming the business world
- Analysis of game-changing sectors like energy, technology and health care
- Strategies of high-performing entrepreneurs

Your future is in our pages.

To see your discount and subscribe go to Forbesmagazine.com/bookoffer.

Forbes